A MEMOIR

Finding THE *Light*

Navigating Dementia with My Son

KASEY J. CLAYTOR

Disclaimer

This book has no specific recommendations for any particular treatment but merely ideas and methods of encouraging good general care for dementia patients. This book does not approve, instruct, or support specific, personal recommendations of any medical or legal direction to individuals. The reader should consider all factors when making informed decisions. Individual situations vary, and this book offers suggestions that may not be appropriate for everyone. Kasey J. Claytor is not legally responsible for medical or care decisions or legal documents made with respect to any information presented in this book or other distribution mediums.

The author of this book does not dispense medical advice or prescribe the use of any technique as a form of treatment for physical, emotional, or medical problems without the advice of a physician, either directly or indirectly. The intent of the author is only to offer information of a general nature to help you in your quest for emotional and spiritual well-being for your loved one and yourself. In the event you use any of the information in this book for yourself, which is your constitutional right, the author and the publisher assume no responsibility for your actions.

© Copyright 2024 Kasey J. Claytor.

All rights reserved. This material may not be duplicated in any way without the express written consent of the publisher, except in the form of brief excerpts or quotations for the purposes of review. The information contained herein is for the personal use of the reader and may not be incorporated into any commercial programs or other books, databases, or any kind of software without written consent of the publisher or author. Making copies of this book, or any portion of it, for any purpose other than your own is a violation of United States copyright laws.

Osprey Publishing

Type Design and Typography: Morin Design

Cover Design: Morin Design and Background Painting by Kasey Claytor

Photo of Author: Robeson Photography

ISBN 979-8-218-47700-4

Printed in the United States of America

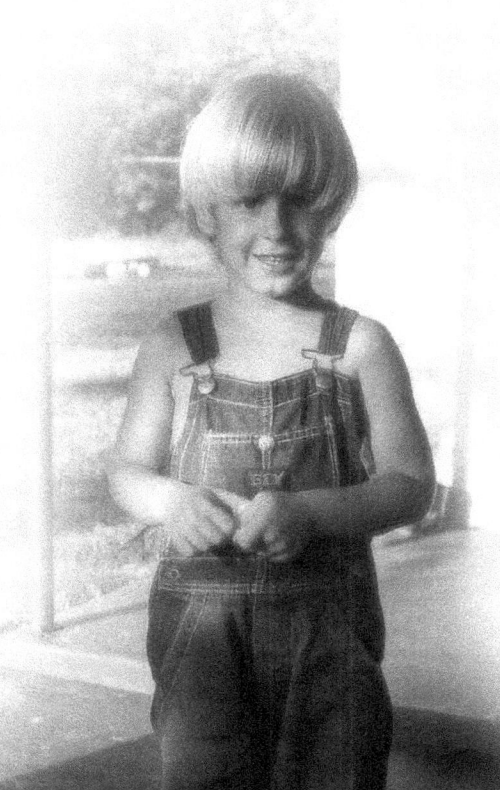

Dedication

*To Justin
My Teacher, Ever-loving Son*

Praise for Finding the Light

"Finding the Light offers a ground-level and personable view into the experience of FTD for all whom it touches. Perhaps more importantly, Claytor provides the crucial reminder of the inherent wholeness that is ever retained in those diagnosed with FTD - witnessed here in the life of her son, Justin. This book serves not as a disembodied manual or how-to guide, but rather as a humane and spiritual reorientation to the gifts in life that will not be limited by the diminishment of cognitive functioning."

–**Rev. Matthew Kern**, MDiv

"I was deeply moved by Justin's journey, as Kasey Claytor depicted in the book. Dalai Lama may see it as a reminder of the frailty of the human condition and the importance of compassion, patience, and love in caring for those who are suffering. It can be an opportunity to practice empathy, kindness, and selflessness in supporting individuals with dementia and their families. Practical advice given to families within this book in similar situations is invaluable."

–**Vijay Jain**, MD, Integrative Medicine physician integrating Ayurveda with modern medicine.

"I first met Justin when I was working as a new nurse. Although his time with us was cut short, he will forever be a positive light in my nursing journey. His love for his mom (BME) and brother, Aaron, was so apparent. Kasey and her family played a pivotal role in Justin's health and well-being;

advocating for him was always their priority. In this memoir, Kasey showcases FTD on a raw, unfiltered, emotional level. This book will be such an eye-opening tool for other families and healthcare professionals!"

–**Danielle Torres**, LPN

"This loving tribute to a challenging and poignant life journey will not only provide a guide to other families who are on this (or similar) journey but also for those who have no experience with dementia, shine a light on what others may be going through and create understanding, tolerance, support, and kindness."

–**Terri Boekhoff**, Retired Family Advisor

This book can be a life changer for those struggling with this kind of challenge who do not have the wherewithal, the higher perspective, or the ability to cope as this author has and see what she can see. As you read, you'll feel the heart of this, the gift of Claytor's story. There is so much valuable information, from practical to spiritual. It's quite a story, and I know that Claytor has navigated this with more grace despite the challenges than most of those who have had this experience. Her story will gift you the ability to navigate your journey with a loved one more easily and gracefully. Her poems are beautiful and would uplift the saddest spirit. This book is such a light.

–**Bonnie Snyder**, Ed. S., CPC, Intuitive Life Balance Coach, and Energy Psychology Diplomate

"This is a valuable resource for anyone on the journey of FTD. Kasey poignantly and honestly lays out the trajectory of her son's diagnosis. While searching for answers, Kasey soon adapts to living her life as it is, not as she thought it would be. The result is that we are now more sensitive, aware, and richer for her story.

> **–Sandi Lutz**, Masters in mental health counseling, M, MHC, AFTD Affiliated Support Group Counselor (retired)

"*Finding the Light* captures the confusion and pain of the FTD journey, but also its moments of tenderness and even joy. Kasey Claytor tells her story with clarity, hope, and a mother's deep love for her son."

> **–Matt Ozga**, AFTD Content Manager

Some stories are impossible to look away from, and from its very first sentence, *Finding the Light, Navigating Dementia with My Son,* by Kasey J. Claytor, proves itself one of them. "...when my 49-year-old son, Justin, was first diagnosed with a form of early-onset dementia, I was stunned." Without hesitation, the book draws readers into a saga of family, illness, and resilience.

Although a memoir, *Finding the Light* is, in many ways, an instructional text. Readers don't need similar medical situations to draw from Claytor's lessons of improvement. The conversational, approachable writing style serves this purpose well.

Finding the Light often feels like a long and enthralling conversation over coffee with a friend.

Between its accessible writing style and the unpredictable medical situation, the book becomes impossible to put down. At each turn, readers will find a surprising development, such as when Justin contends with COVID or when he must repeatedly move to new facilities. And each development is carefully contextualized with compassion for Justin, his caretakers, and everybody touched by the impacts of FTD. A literary rhythm emerges: touching scene, thoughtful reflection, clear information.

Thanks to *Finding the Light*, readers will have a roadmap for traveling through whatever dark paths life has in store with grace, acceptance, and love.

– Chanticleer Book Reviews

In her poignant memoir *Finding the Light: Navigating Dementia with My Son*, Kasey Claytor confronts the devastating reality of her son Justin's diagnosis of Frontotemporal Degeneration (FTD). At the heart of this narrative are profound themes of love and resilience that shape both the author's and Justin's experiences. Claytor's tone is one of raw honesty interspersed with moments of tenderness; she shares insights into her tumultuous journey with a heart grounded in love for her son while struggling with the harsh realities of his condition. The adjustments she must make to create an environment where her son can evolve with a strong sense of self-worth are captured in detail. This memoir offers an irresistible premise — a mother's discovery that her 49-year-old son has early-onset dementia.

Linguistically, Claytor employs vivid imagery that illustrates her feelings in the moments spent with Justin. Descriptive passages capture not just the mundane aspects of caregiving but also the joyful moments, like Justin's celebratory 'yeses' to simple pleasures and his unconditional love for those around him. The language she uses shifts seamlessly from the clinical vocabulary that pervades discussions of dementia to the tender dialogues shared between mother and son, creating an intimate portrait of their life together.

Finding the Light explores the broader implications of caregiving and the societal attitudes surrounding dementia. Through her experiences, Claytor emphasizes the importance of compassion over judgment, especially considering the human reactions people with dementia can evoke. The central message underlines that beyond the disease and its symptoms lies a person deserving of dignity, love, and understanding. Kasey's insistence on finding "the light" in their journey provides hope to others enduring similar struggles, affirming that love can illuminate a path forward even amid the darkness. This memoir is filled with light, insight, and love. It is a story of motherhood and humanity that will capture the hearts of many readers.

– 5 Stars The Book Commentary

Other Books by Kasey Claytor

Fiction
The God of Anna (Under the name of Kasey Greenhoe)
The Light of Grace

Children's Books
Pinky and the Magical Secret He Kept Inside

Poetry
I know...Me Too

Non-Fiction
The 7 Laws of Raising Financially Independent Kids
Spiritual Will & Legacy
The Money Map, A Spiritual Guide for Financial Success

Author Biography

Claytor has over thirty years of experience in the investment and financial advisory business, counseling clients on retirement, college funding, estate wealth transfer, and wealth building. In 2000, she formed Osprey Money Management, LLC, an independent financial advisory service that she now runs with her son, Aaron. She has also written two financial books: *The Money Map, A Spiritual Guide for Financial Success,* and *The 7 Laws of Raising Financially Independent Kids.*

She believes that the power to grow in self-knowledge and awareness makes desired situations possible, and her mission is to guide others toward transformation into their true selves. As a lifelong meditator, she's earned the certification as a meditation instructor through the Chopra Center for Wellbeing in Carlsbad, CA. She is also an Ayurvedic consultant, a five-thousand-year-old body of knowledge in the health sciences. She has studied methods to enrich, enliven, and bring well-being to her readers, meditation students, and clients.

As an experienced public speaker, she has spoken at conferences such as the Florida Conference for Women, the Vibrant Women's Conference, and the Florida Association of Women Attorneys. Some of her presentations include "Women and Prosperity," "Meditation," "The Map of Money Consciousness," and "Power vs. Force."

Her books have won awards from Chanticleer Reviews and Foreword Reviews, among others. The Money

Map and Pinky, a children's book, received first place in their category.

Her website, kaseyclaytor.com, has a resources page, a recommended reading list, a money map quiz, a blog, and a sign-up for her three emails: very brief, inspirational Phoenix Messages for Passionate Extraordinary Living; Osprey Money Management Newsletter on investing confidently in today's complicated world; and Prosperity and Wellbeing Newsletter, with news and dynamic mind/body/spirit articles.

She lives on the East Coast of Florida with her husband and dog, Max.

Finding
THE
Light

Table of Contents

Introduction, Page 17

Chapter 1: 2019, Page 21

Chapter 2: 2020, Page 27

Chapter 3: 2021, Page 47

Chapter 4: 2022, Page 85

Chapter 5: 2023, Page 113

Epilogue, Page 133

Acknowledgments, Page 135

Bibliography, Page 139

Introduction

Writing can be a form of therapy for me, yet when my 49-year-old son, Justin, was first diagnosed with a form of early-onset dementia, I was stunned. Writing about it wasn't even on my radar. Moving through the day with many tasks—taking him to the doctor, researching, and planning our future around this shock—would take all of my energy.

Initially, it felt as though my mental abilities were failing for several reasons. I wasn't myself. I had become forgetful, and I wasn't as present with others outside of my shrinking world because I was so focused on my son and his condition. I found myself in scary situations, like driving on the wrong side of a one-way street. I thought, *Was I trying to harm myself? Why would I be so careless?*

As the months passed, we slowly adjusted to a new life routine. I became more accustomed to a new vision of life and how it would be. I had been planning on slowing down at work. My husband was already retired. We had plans to travel more, enjoying the fruits of our long careers.

The first two years after my son's diagnosis, Justin was ok staying in his home nearby. The neurologist gave him tests to make sure he could still drive. His employer finally had to let him go. His wife was a traveling nurse, so I checked on him often. But, in due course, my son's wife left, which is common in this situation. When a spouse no longer recognizes their affected mate, it has to be devastating. It's frightening when someone you love changes so radically. Taking care of him fell on me, which felt natural as his mother—it was like he was becoming my little boy again.

After adjusting as much as possible, I started emailing updates to friends and family about Justin's condition and letting them know how he was doing. I also kept copies of my communications with doctors and others involved in his care, creating a treasure trove of knowledge as we navigated this journey.

I still often read posts on a Facebook support group from people dealing with loved ones suffering from Frontotemporal Degeneration. There's so much pain and uncertainty with this disease: no known cause, no known cure. If sharing our experiences and small successes can ease some of the pain, I want to help.

This compilation of communications includes added explanations to provide knowledge and support to others who may face a similar journey.

I had a few advantages that helped me through this journey. With over 40 years as a financial advisor and planner, I knew what I needed to do legally and financially to protect my son.

I also spent 25 years as a certified meditation instructor and teacher of the Chopra Center's course, Perfect Health, based on Ayurveda, which originates from the same sources as yoga. This course provided advice for finding wholeness and well-being with gentle suggestions for a daily routine, stress reduction practices, and tips for regaining balance. It helped Justin and the rest of us, especially in the early months.

Finding the Light

Lastly, looking at the facts and hard reality of this journey, you will see a sad story. Delving deeper and finding its mystical or spiritual side can offer hope, where the person with dementia finds happiness, even a sense of well-being, with gratitude for simply being. Those around them can learn how to create the conditions that make this more likely.

There are always deeper truths to a story. Seeing this situation only on the surface is quite dire. We have many perspectives or ways of framing a problem in our experience. We can become bogged down in the minutiae of endless tasks caring for someone with dementia, or we can find the light coming from within us and our loved ones—guiding us to the lessons and the beauty beneath.

Note: The boxed text is my current, added information and comments.

May All Beings Be Released from Suffering

Chapter 1: 2019

August 21, 2019
Four Months After Diagnosis

My son, Justin, has always been an enigma. Brilliant yet with learning disabilities, drawn to the spiritual side of life with an innate sense for understanding other people and their psychological states, high inter- and intra-personal intelligence, yet like most of our family, difficulty learning in the way our culture teaches. Well-read in world religions but often foggy-headed, we always thought he got a double dose of the family learning problems.

  This past year or so, my other son, Aaron, and I have talked about how Justin was more than his usual foggy-headed and uncharacteristically extraverted at family functions. Then, in April, Aaron got a phone call from one of his friends who worked with his brother. He said they were worried about Justin. He had been acting differently. Then, this co-worker overheard one of the managers talking about how they would meet with personnel regarding his work and ask him to come in. That started it. Plus, his memory was getting bad.

  Thank God for my friends. One is a yoga teacher and an EMT, and she and her husband, a physician, have a medical triage software business. Another friend is a surgeon and an

Ayurvedic physician. Both of them told me to have Justin get a CT scan ASAP. The only way to do that quickly was to drive him to the emergency room and tell them he had a noticeable personality change, and the family was concerned. His wife, a traveling nurse, was working out of town, so I let her know.

After Justin couldn't answer the hospital staff's questions, such as who was president, they did a CT scan and kept him overnight. They were worried about the results and wanted to do an MRI and a contrasting CT scan the following day.

Some brain shrinkage, as aging can do at 49, and a small older lesion on his frontal lobe. The neurologist didn't think it was enough to cause his symptoms and suggested ADHD and depression. I didn't think that was right.

He went back to work at the Kennedy Space Center, and his symptoms worsened. Soon he got his ID badge taken away temporarily, meaning he wasn't allowed back on the base. His company then ran him through their tests.

I took him back to the neurologist, who ran him through psych tests, and also a psychologist who diagnosed Frontal Lobe dementia and said he shouldn't drive or work. Justin kept saying he was fine. His wife and I took him to my friend, who is a doctor, and I researched on my own. My notes at that time:

1. Ayurvedic physician says he has an imbalance, and it will take about a year to heal his brain. His brain is affected by his repressed anger. After his appointment, Justin experienced a dose of compassion and hope,

and he improved immensely. He is carefully following the doctor's recommendations.
2. A Chopra counselor said he is entering a period of withdrawal in his astrology chart, and that can mean many things.
3. I've heard that Alzheimer's is buried anger, and dementia is a wish to be cared for.
4. At the last neurologist appointment, she said she wanted Justin to see a psychologist to learn how to express his anger and not shut down. He shuts down when people keep questioning him. He is an introvert; he has never shown any tendency to be cruel, unkind, etc. My Buddha boy. He loves nature, the National Geographic channel, caring for their animals, etc. I am skeptical that a psychologist would be helpful for someone with a brain that is shrinking and cannot reason or remember well.
5. Another Counselor, looking at Justin's situation, thinks that Justin is lonely because his ambitious wife works so much. She is a tiger lady who is trying her best for him.

So, here we are. I keep thinking, where did I mess up? What did I do wrong? He was born two weeks late. Should I have made the doctor induce? He had severe colic. I was all alone with him when his father was in Vietnam. I was too young and didn't have enough patience. He was rebellious at times growing up. I even spanked him a couple of times; I never thought I'd do that—my fault. Yet, I read every book on child care, got him into a preschool co-op at the college where the parents went to classes, etc.

We had learning disabilities on both sides of our families. UGH, I don't know. It is all unknown what will happen. I move through life aware of a new landscape before me when in my ego, my outward-focused self, and it's depressing. Then, I somehow manage to flip to my inner self and know for a time that it is all okay.

I've also read on support groups of family members saying, "My loved one isn't there anymore." But somewhere deep inside, they still are; pay attention to the emotions, if they can still emote. If not, you need to seek even deeper until you can sense the essence of that person because, I believe, their soul and the divine are still holding that body in perfect, infinite love.

> Justin had a type of FTD that affects personality and behavior, called bvFTD or Behavioral Variant. There are also other types: Primary Progressive Non-Fluent Aphasia, which affects speech, and Semantic Dementia, which affects language and understanding. A less common form, Motor Neurone Disease, FTD-MND, affects movement similar to ALS or Parkinson's.
>
> All types are terminal.
>
> In addition, please know that no fault lies with a parent or spouse that would cause this illness to occur. It's normal for us to try to find reasons, but sometimes, there isn't one.

Eventually I had to learn to trust myself, trust in my own research, and my own decisions.

11-17-2019
To My Ayurvedic Doctor Friend

It was so helpful to meet with you on Friday. I was much more relaxed and felt up to the meeting I had later with Justin's wife. She was sorry she had withdrawn from the family. She told me it has been all she can do to keep together in the present, and she was overwhelmed trying to think forward. She cried several times. She told me it was hard for her to be with Justin for long periods. It is hard for all of us to be around him for long periods. She feels so anxious that she has to be alone to put herself back into a functioning state. She hasn't been able to sleep without sleeping pills this whole time. (She needs to see you.)

I told her we understood and would not judge her, whatever decision she made. It is a tough position, and we will step up and take care of Justin anytime. She told me she feels more comfortable with me handling Justin's money. I think they had issues with his and her money in the past.

After that meeting, she said she loved me and thanked me. She said she felt so much better having talked to me. She has been with Justin ever since. I'm unsure where it is going now, though I feel much better. We now

Kasey J. Claytor

have a better line of communication. My communication was from my better self, and my anger was gone.

-Kasey

> I did find that first year, throughout Justin's home, post-it notes his wife left, stuck everywhere, on cabinets and walls, reminding Justin of various things to do around the house.
>
> He also developed a habit of writing in a journal daily about what he did, how his dog was, what he ate, and what he was grateful for! I can barely pick it up now without tearing up. How brilliant of him.

Chapter 2: 2020

January 31, 2020

I am going to Justin's almost every day. It is becoming apparent that he isn't capable of handling the mail, taking care of bills, etc. I went through a massive pile of mail on his desk, and in it was Justin's neurological referral from the University of Florida's Department of Neurology in Gainesville from November, critical insurance information, unopened bills, and statements from first glance. Justin's wife is gone most of the time as a traveling nurse.

Justin's needs are growing and not being met. I wish this weren't so. I must be more involved if she isn't going to. He will likely need home care, a legal trust, a power of attorney, plans set up, medical services, insurance, and estate planning—all these things that a spouse usually takes care of.

I changed Justin's previous employer's address to my office so we won't miss anything, and I've received his W2 and termination papers.

I applied for disability for Justin with his company, and he was approved and then denied! I went to the neurologist's office (took three times), got the requested information to appeal the cancellation, and sent it off with a letter asking them to please reinstate the benefit. I've spent about 10 hours with phone calls and paperwork this past week.

Many people don't know where to begin when a loved one becomes mentally disabled. Part of my job as a financial planner is making sure my clients have their family documents completed for the possibility of something like this happening. Anytime a husband, wife, parent, or grandparent becomes incapable of making decisions, signing documents, selling property, or performing other life tasks, someone must be named to take this job over. It is usually a spouse or child, but it could be any trusted person who can carry out these duties.

What must be taken over for the person with FTD:

- bill paying,
- handling insurance filing,
- applying for aid or Medicare,
- Social Security Disability Insurance,
- medical decisions,
- real estate transactions and banking,
- brokerage accounts,
- retirement accounts

Note here that the Social Security Administration can fast-track applications for Social Security Disability Insurance, or SSDI, for someone with a dementia diagnosis. When I applied for Justin, they were kind and efficient. We had approval in a few short weeks, and it was retroactive to when his diagnosis was made.

Documents the family needs:

- Durable Power of Attorney, DPOA

- Health Care Surrogate
- Will
- Trust (optional)

(Note: the names of these documents may be different from state to state.)

I recommend seeing an estate planning attorney for details. If assets owned by the person suffering from FTD are limited, and you consider yourself capable of handling this yourself, you could go to a legal documents site or a para-legal for a significantly lower cost.

My son was good with his money. He saved like crazy. He added few thousand each year from his savings to invest. He contributed the maximum to his company retirement account. He paid off his mortgage. Because of this, when he became sick, he was afforded the best care available. This was one potential disaster we wouldn't face. And a lesson for everyone: save for retirement and save for the future.

I plan to call the University of Florida to schedule an appointment for Justin. They have an excellent neurology department. My son, Aaron, wants to go with me too.

To the Neurologist: Update on Justin Wade's behavior/condition as of June 8, 2020:

1. He is still driving well, but we know it needs to be addressed soon. It is his one pleasurable and soothing activity, such as going for a river road drive. We fear it will be a significant hurdle

for him to give up driving, especially because he lives alone. (We live around the corner.)
2. In the last several weeks, he's begun to need prompting to shave, change into clean clothes, do the laundry, and feed and water his chickens. He is occasionally resistant when I try to help; for example, once, when I tried to fill the dog bowl, he grabbed it out of my hand.
3. He has a caregiver three days a week and a dementia nurse who spends two or three hours a week assessing him, giving him exercises, etc.
4. He adheres rigidly to his morning routine of making oatmeal, coffee, medication, etc.
5. He often texts all of us in the family and his caregiver. He puts everything on his phone calendar so he always knows who is coming and when.
6. I took his motorcycle keys, and he keeps wanting to order a replacement key, thinking he lost them. But he is beginning to realize he isn't going to ride it anymore. We have told him it is too dangerous out in traffic lately.
7. His wife is divorcing him, though he does not know yet. She has been working primarily out of town for two years and is presently in Maryland. She will continue to call and text him, but I have no idea what she tells him. She told me she wanted to continue to visit him. We all act like she is still his wife, and he doesn't seem worried. We are concerned about how he will be when it sinks in.

June 15, 2020
Today Justin is OK

Today Justin is ok
Today he's proud of the independence he has
Today he has a routine he's comfortable with
Today he has a great support system
Today he isn't in any pain
Today

When it first sunk in
This unbelievable condition
My world shifted as much as
Suddenly being blinded
I could not see the world as it had been
It was a new scary place
I didn't belong here
Lost in a land of constant discomfort

Aha~
The guilt that remains
Mistakes made
From the raising of a child
Revisits
Until it's rectification
In my mind
Toward the path
Of ultimate self-forgiveness.

Kasey J. Claytor

July 20, 2020
MRI Results and Doctor's Appointment

- The MRI is good news. There was no further atrophy. He is holding strong.
- He has gained about 12 pounds in the last six weeks. With Frontotemporal Degeneration, they often crave sugar and carbs. The doctor explained the harm of sugar to his brain function, the harm of more than two hours of TV a day, and lack of exercise. But getting him to comply with cutting back on sugar and TV and getting exercise has been extremely difficult.
- He is doing much better keeping his dog Basil's water clean and filled, the chickens watered and fed, and Basil fed. A few months ago, he was so lethargic that he forgot to do these things. I think what helped him was a combination of repetitive reminding and taking him off the donepezil, which he should have never been prescribed. (It is for Alzheimer's, and his neurologist should not have prescribed it.) Of course, the animal care falls to me.
- He doesn't show irritation or stubbornness like he used to. I think this is partly due to discontinuing the wrong medication, his anti-inflammatory supplements, and his diet and partly to our growing understanding of his perspective. We are learning not to contradict or question him much and to try to use his emotional responses as a guide.

Justin seems primarily happy, but he's resistant to changing his routines. For example, he puts his 'clean' dishes in the dishwasher but never runs it, and when he hand-washes dishes, he doesn't use soap. I have to run the dishwasher after him. It's challenging for him when I try to change his habits, but I'm learning to adapt.

I hired a caregiver to stay with him while I worked, but she quit after a few weeks. She said Justin sits in his chair and watches TV the whole time she's there, and she doesn't think she's needed. We'll try going without a caregiver for a while.

I'm learning a lot about caring for someone with a brain disease. I've been reading *"Contented Dementia"* and watching videos by Teepa Snow, a caregiving instructor for dementia patients. I've learned that their emotional life remains unchanged, but their thinking can be affected, leading to strong frustrations. It's essential to observe their emotions and take cues from them.

With FTD, they usually retain long-term memories of people, which is different from Alzheimer's.

Justin's wife has taken an apartment in a nearby city. I'd like her to tell me when she will visit and if she discusses divorce. Last time, her sudden visit caught us off guard, and I could have adjusted the caregiver's schedule to give her privacy.

Lately, Justin has been getting upset when his wife visits. With his big blue eyes, he looks up from the couch and asks me questions about her. I don't know how to respond because I don't know what she's told him. He gets depressed and worries if she'll ever live with him again. It's heart-wrenching to see him like this. Once she leaves, he'll be okay with it after a couple of days.

I believe it's time for her to make a clear decision so Justin can heal instead of remaining in this uncertain state. Her calls and texts confuse him, and they're keeping him worried. I just want my son to feel good about himself and be happy.

September 2020

This past year, I've been fighting reality on this planet, wanting my old life back where I didn't need to worry daily about a family member's struggles, activities, or condition. This constant worry was a form of prison in which I thought I might never figure out how to escape. I'd have moments—periods I felt 'normal' again—but it was temporary. This worry was so large that every other worry morphed into an inconsequentially small one.

In these windows of sanity, I would take time to research, ponder, and meditate, and then a bit more moments where my thinking became clearer between my feelings of overwhelming angst, and I finally began to see slivers of light.

I found some poignant posts in a Facebook support group. Still, a large amount of the posts would express how bad it is, how the disease is horrible, how their loved one is gone from them, and how many of the loved ones are suffering from irritability, depression, and anger. Most agree it is tough.

My son is usually well, loves attention, and still has moments of clarity. His has been a slow onset over the last few years, with a diagnosis a year and a half ago. He wasn't always this way, though; he would sometimes become down, irritable, and stubborn. That was before we learned a different way to be around him.

Think of his perspective. Think of the courage to wake up every day and know you are deficient and forgetful; thinking has become so hard. But you don't understand why. It feels bad. But you arise and enter the day, not knowing or understanding what it may hold. That's courage.

People may ask you questions that you can't answer. Or tell you you've done something wrong, or you hear depressing news, yet you can't come up with words about how that makes you feel. But you still go about your day as best you can.

I am learning new caregiving skills. By no means am I perfect, but little by little, I am changing my behavior to elicit well-being in my son.

The straightforward, modern treatment has been to keep the patient clean, well-fed, happy, and occupied, if possible. The solution is often trying various pharmaceuticals for any difficult behavior that prevents this. I'm not denying that sometimes it is warranted, especially when the patient presents a danger to himself or others. However, I am often surprised by how many drugs some of these patients are on. Some have horrendous side effects.

I am also surprised how some psychiatrists think making these patients 'face reality,' even though they will forget, is helpful. I read a post from a son whose mother is in a facility and keeps asking to go home. (This, of course, is so common.) Her psychiatrist told her son she needed to 'face reality' and be told the house was sold! Imagine reliving her hurt every time she hears this, needing to be told this over and over. Instead, she could be told, oh, the house had a plumbing accident, it is in such a mess, it isn't livable right now. She could accept this and have a sense of well-being.

This idea came from a new method for caregivers, detailed in the book *Contented Dementia* by Oliver James. It was developed by an intuitive woman, Penny, who noticed her mother with dementia had a sense of well-being when she was with her, but Mom was difficult and irritated when she was with Dad. Dad was a doctor and didn't want to accept that his wife had dementia. He badgered her with questions and insisted she could remember. He tried to control her.

Conversely, when Mom was with Penny, Penny would study her reactions and feelings, attempting to view things from her perspective. For example, when Penny visited her mom when she was placed in an assisted living cottage, upon saying she had to go home, her mom cried terribly. She discovered it was the word 'home.'

Her mother wanted to go home, too. Penny switched to, "I have to go pick up some things at the store, and I will be back tomorrow. Is there anything that you would like me to bring you?" Her mother accepted this easily. No more tears!

There is a lot more in this new method, but the basis is this: Yes, memory (and personality) are affected in bvFTD, but the person's emotions are still 100% felt.

Penny discovered she could help patients tap into their well-being when she understood their emotions. Even someone with deficient memory can be content.

With my son, I try not to ask him a battery of questions but rather poke around the topic with statements. He isn't pressured to try to come up with an answer, which can make him think he failed if the answer isn't available.

In the past, I'd ask him, "What did you have for lunch?" he would look blankly at me while he searched his mind for the information. Usually, it wouldn't come, and his face would fall.

When someone with dementia feels good about himself, more information is available. The stress is gone. If I say while looking in the fridge, "Boy, you have lots of great meals to choose from. I'll bet you're full," he'll often respond, miraculously, telling me what he had. I wasn't demanding he remember anything. Out of feeling good, the memory was offered up.

Getting him to do his chores (being physically active is helpful for him) was difficult before. Now, not so much. This morning, I saw some limbs lying in the yard and said, "I'm going to take these branches down to a pile on the road. I think the truck is coming today. I could use some help."

He popped right up to help. In the past, I would've asked him, "Will you pick up the fronds and limbs in the yard and get them down to the road today?" He'd say yes, that he'd do it, and then it would never get done.

I wrote this to myself around this time. 'His constant validation of me and expressions that I am doing OK as his mother seems, to me, from beyond. God knows my feelings of guilt and worry. Am I being sent messages through Justin?

Justin is becoming my teacher—ever loving and forgiving, no matter what I do or say. I am so imperfect as a parent. In his apparent illness, he is a genius; he is 'light.'

At this time, my husband is stocking Justin's refrigerator with ready meals. We buy all his supplies, take care of the animals, and often have him over for dinner. I come by daily, and Aaron makes it over at least once a week.

My husband's sister is also making trips over to spend time with him, watching his game shows with him. He loves seeing her.

We are in a flow now. Justin has a routine that makes him happy. He is proud of the routine he's devised to remember to take his pills. I count out the medicine and supplements daily to make sure he takes them as prescribed, knowing I will need to take over that job eventually.

Here is what I typed up for him (based on my Ayurvedic studies):

Justin's Mighty Awesome Plan to Reveal His Most Fierce Amazing Self Every Morning After Coffee take:

- 1 Tablespoon of the Brahmi Rasayana Jam
- Take 2 Healthy Pitta Tablets with warm water at breakfast, lunch, and dinner
- Make a big thermos of CCF tea every day and sip throughout the day:
    - 2 Tablespoons cumin, coriander, and fennel tea seeds from the bag
    - Fill a small pot with water and add seeds
    - Bring to a boil and simmer for 5 minutes

OR

- Follow doctor's instructions with the ground spices of cumin, coriander and fennel
- May add some honey

He loves telling me his routine, especially how he prepares his coffee each night before bed, so all he needs to do is turn the coffee machine on in the morning. Everything now is on repeat. I happily listen, cherishing the moments because one day it will stop, and I will miss these times.

I still have a video of him explaining how he prepares his coffee for the next day.

He also loves his game shows and the home video shows. He knows the air times, and if he happens to be over at our home when one comes on, he rushes home to watch.

September 16, 2020

I brought Justin to our family doctor last Monday, and he is a perfect specimen physically, with blood pressure, heart rate, etc. I had to spell out some things about his condition in front of him, which I hate to do because he doesn't want to hear it, but he still understood and was unhappy as we left.

When we were driving home, though, he soon forgot, and we sang along with the radio! One of the 'benefits' (or challenges) of his condition is the loss of inhibitions, which frees him up to sing and dance to his heart's content. He used to be self-conscious.

We've been concerned for Justin's dog, Basil, a Catahoula leopard mix. The dog isn't high maintenance except for some medications for his allergies, but it was stressful for me to check daily to see if Justin gave him the meds, fed him, took him out, etc. Another effect of FTD is losing the ability to experience empathy and growing apathy. He does show some of that, such as not petting Basil or paying attention to him; he would even push him away. All of us who came by Justin's, including his caregivers, gave Basil attention, but I felt terrible for the dog. In preparation for the eventual need to find a place for Basil, I began preparing Justin a few weeks ago, making up a story that I had a friend who lived alone and wanted a big dog to keep her company and protect her.

Last week, a friend offered to help me do some work at Justin's house. The first time she came in, Basil acted like he knew her! He wouldn't leave her side! On another visit, she asked if she could take him home for a few days because she felt so bonded with him. Also, she was alone and would love company and protection and go on walks with him! We talked with Justin about it, and he said that's fine! He was OK with it. (After all, I'd been telling him that story!)

Finding the Light

This week, she texted Justin and me how Basil was doing—great. I asked Justin, "What if she wants to keep him?" I waited to hear what he would say. He said, "That's fine!" with a smile. It is another perfect resolution with no conflict. It's so interesting how things fall into place.

Below is a poem written by Cindy Odell, a long-time member of the AFTD Persons with FTD Advisory Council. In it, she expresses her profound frustrations with her FTD diagnosis. The poem ends with a powerful reminder that people with FTD are still, in fact, people and no less deserving of respect than anyone else.

I am so very tired.
Tired of this disease of FTD stealing all my energy.
Tired of falling.
Tired of hurting.
Tired of forgetting, mid-sentence, what I am saying...
and not remembering.
Tired of people judging me for the things I can no longer do, no longer remember.
Tired of people not celebrating the things I do accomplish.
Tired of seeing rolling eyes.
Tired of being ignored.
Tired of debilitating headaches.
Tired of medications not helping.
Tired of not being trusted to be alone with children or animals.
Tired of having to rely on others for everything.

> Tired of people taking over because I am doing something too slowly or not the "right" way.
> Tired of doctors addressing the person with me instead of me.
> Tired of people not speaking with me because "I won't understand."
> Tired of having no energy.
> Tired, just tired... always tired.
> Please, I AM STILL HERE!
>
> *(Reprinted with permission from the author.)*

November 2020
Update for Neighbors

Dear Friends and Neighbors,

I recently had a long conversation with two experts about Justin and whether what we are doing for him is enough, not enough, or just right. We now have a GPS tracker on his truck. He dearly loves to take his daily drive down Tropical Trail along the river and his trips to Walmart and Publix. This is his routine. His driving is still OK. I watch his speed on each trip, where he goes, and when.

What has been a bit frustrating to me is hiring 'companions' to be with him and keep him company while I am at work, encouraging him to move, and making sure he eats the meals we set up for him, etc. But, as it turns out, even when a caregiver is there, he may get up and go to the store!

Therefore, I sought counsel from a theaftd.org trained caregiver and support leader, Sandi, to decide if employing these helpers is premature. I described Justin's behavior, routine, and the fact that he is still somewhat independent. I told her what we are doing for him and how our friends and family are stepping up to help in wonderful ways. (My sister-in-law cleaning the chicken coop and spending time with him and his interests, to a girlfriend going for a bike ride with him and giving him a massage, to my husband, Bill, conscientiously stocking excellent food choices in Justin's refrigerator, Aaron taking afternoons to visit him, and of course, my daily visits to check on him and everything at his house.) It is so appreciated; you could never know how much!

We also have a set monthly visit with a dementia nurse who takes him out for lunch and drives.

We hired a caregiver for four hours twice a week but have now realized, after talking with the experts, that it was premature. Justin asked why someone had come and just sat on the couch. I also told her about his behavior. He still, as he has for the last two years, occasionally breaks out in dance when he is happy, might begin singing, and sometimes will poke someone. This is 'normal' of the behavioral variant of FTD. As the AFTD counselor said, this is as good as it gets; enjoy every moment because it will change. He is still in the beginning stage.

She also explained that if we remove the truck and stop his driving too prematurely, he will become frustrated and irritated. If we wait, the change will hopefully go smoothly because he will likely accept it. I realize it will be sooner rather than later, but abruptly taking away his little independence before it is necessary is cruel.

His brain is slowly dying, and it will eventually cause his death, so we need to allow every bit of happiness he can experience and enjoy our time with him now. Under the watchful eye of our friend, an MD using Ayurvedic knowledge, we are hopefully slowing down the progression, I believe, reducing the inflammation and helping nudge him to more well-being. The emphasis now is on his feelings, his emotional life, and doing everything possible to reduce stressors.

I'm also learning so much about the effects of being judgmental. Justin's behavior is odd at times. When we see someone behaving in a way that we don't usually, we may think he or she looks crazy, be repelled, criticize, or think they are funny.

This morning, while driving down our street, I saw a man on a bike, wearing clothes that aren't 'proper' for bike riding—sort of baggy and sloppy—with a huge, messy basket of sticks on the back and a wide smile on his face. Before Justin's illness, I may have judged him, but I smiled back at him, understanding that he could be someone like my son, feeling happy. This is one of the many gifts I've received through this experience.

Some people may be put off by his friendliness, willingness to share, and happy dancing, but he means well. He told me this morning how important it is to be a good person.

Finding the Light

Around this time, I learned the theaftd.org site has a template for an ID card with room for his photo that says, "I have a brain disease. If I appear to need assistance, Please Call...I downloaded it and had it printed up on a card with my cell number and his photo.

He didn't like it when I put it in his wallet. He kept taking it out, but I told him it was for his safety and that they would call my number if he needed anything. Finally, he gave up and allowed it to be in his wallet.

One day, I got a call. It said police department on the ID. I answered. They said, "We are in the Publix shopping center, and we're talking to Justin Wade. He keeps telling us his driver's license number. We found the card and just want to check and see if he is OK."

I told them I was his mom and, yes, he was OK. He is proud to know his driver's license number. His neurologist said he is OK to drive. Thank you for taking the time to find out. I told them a bit about FTD, and we hung up. We have great police.

I knew his driving would need to be stopped eventually. I wasn't looking forward to that.

Chapter 3: 2021

January 2021

There is very little change with Justin right now. Of course, I see him daily, so that subtle changes may be under my radar. He smiles and expresses gratitude profusely, which is nice to be around.

It occurred to me that the aggression some caregivers report on my FTD Facebook group isn't one of Justin's symptoms because we 'spoil' him! As we've learned from researching FTD, telling them they are wrong, correcting them, or arguing with them is counter-productive. Therefore, we go along with whatever he says as much as possible. It isn't easy; most people have a knee-jerk reaction to correct them. Yet some afflicted with FTD may be aggressive no matter what the caregivers do.

Imagine you are becoming extremely forgetful, but you are mostly unaware of it, and the people around you constantly disagree with you, arguing with you, telling you that you did something you have no memory of, that you are wrong, or that you didn't do what you were supposed to do? You would feel badly at the least and irate at most. Dementia patients may not remember what was said or what they did or you did, but they store all of their feelings intact. This storage of feelings is tapped every time they experience that emotion. When irritated or ashamed, it connects to the storage within of all the other times they felt that way, and it can be overwhelming. They don't know where this comes from.

On the other hand, if they tap into their good feelings and you learn how to foster this, it can make all the difference in the world. Lately, Justin has been talking about his dad a lot. He passed away in 1997. Justin brings visitors to his desk, where he has a large photo of Dad, and smiles profusely, telling them about him. Almost every day, he tells me that his dad has been sending him messages. This morning, he told me he could *feel Dad's smile inside* as he laid his hand on his chest! He had told me this way before the FTD. His eyes tear up, and his smile is blissful. He has tapped into all the *good* feelings he has stored within.

This is a progressive disease, and I try, with the desire to blanket him with a protective barrier, to prevent all possible problems medically, financially, and environmentally and prepare ahead for all possible effects of this disease. Looking back at what I did last year, I pre-emptively hired a home care service when he could still care for himself with daily supervision. His feelings of freedom and self-responsibility are massively important to him.

We have an independent living apartment reserved for him in a brand-new, state-of-the-art facility that includes assisted living and memory care. He is a bit young right now to be accepted in assisted living, but if he can continue like he is for a couple more years, he will be eligible.

That is one of the biggest tragedies of this disease. There are no facilities for young FTD sufferers right now. Since it is so rare, it doesn't catch the eye of providers or developers. There are a few Traumatic Brain Injury living centers spread around the country, which is also a possibility. I have to give a shout-out to *A Place for Mom*. Someone recommended them, and Terri, our advisor, has been excellent, working constantly with me on a good plan. I had thought APFM was just for seniors, but it is for anyone with dementia-related illness who needs living arrangements. (There used to be mental hospitals, but with a bad reputation and the ACLU challenging the legality of locking people up against their will, they have gone by the wayside, and nothing has ever replaced them. Today, I'm afraid people with mental illness, dementia, and FTD are a big segment of the homeless population.)

I told you that in the past, we found a wonderful home for Basil, Justin's dog, and recently, our nephew, Todd, has managed the future problem of the dear chickens and found a good place for them. I am so grateful and proud of my family. Everyone has been so helpful; I don't know what I would have done without them all.

> Many loved ones of FTD patients take care of them at home. Sometimes, this works out fine; the relatives become caregivers and have managed to provide for all their needs. It can be deeply rewarding. However, I've noticed that this isn't always the best solution, both for the caregiver and the FTDer.
>
> The loved one may be unpredictable, unaware of the dangers posed to them, and can't be watched at home

24 hours a day. In support groups, I've read about them getting up in the middle of the night and leaving the house, soiling themselves, gorging themselves, taking the car, driving up charges online, even having affairs, etc.

This causes terrible rifts in the family, destroying any peaceful existence at home. Our history with our relatives brings out our emotional reactions to any of these events, further causing friction. The loved one will likely balk at any reprimand for destructive, dangerous, or unhealthy behavior.

We considered bringing Justin into our home during his illness. But we had no way to lock him inside or keep him away from all food, no way to stop him from going back to his own house around the corner.

When he was riding his bike down the street, he would stop and talk to everyone. One day a neighbor observed him stop and hop off his bike to say hi to a couple working in their front yard. The husband quickly turned his wife toward the house and told her sharply to go inside.

This made me so sad, but it also brought to my awareness the dangers of allowing Justin free reign. We decided to have him in assisted living, where he could not leave yet had ample room to explore and participate in various activities—things to keep him occupied. It was the best practical choice for all of us.

When the Brain Won't Oblige
By Kasey Claytor

It's alarming
That's true
When the brain won't oblige
You can't remember
What was just said
You have to change
How you do things
Writing down the happenings
Each day
Until you can't remember
to do even that

So, you take photos
With your phone
What you ate
Who you saw
Where you went
And with who
Hundreds of photos
And you still smile
All the time

Because you are naturally
In the present moment
In every moment
Not weighed down

Kasey J. Claytor

By societal mores
Such as how you look,
How you sound

You don't judge others
You accept everyone
And assume they mean well
And you are peaceful
You consistently find
The silver lining
And treat all equally
You've accepted your fate

And we don't know how
But we let you be
Don't disagree
Because you are always right

People looking in
From their regular lives
Think it's horrible
What's happened to you
In fact, they feel sorry for you

We feel sorry for them
Those who don't see you
Our Buddha boy

You are teaching us.

I've read that driving can lower stress. Think about how, when you're upset, taking a scenic drive can help. We live along the river, part of the Intracoastal Waterway on the East Coast of Florida. It is beautiful. Justin would take a drive practically every day, riding along the river road, crossing the causeways to the beaches on A1A south, and then taking another causeway back up to our neighborhood.

I watched him on my app connected to the GPS monitor we hid in his car. One day, he showed me a traffic ticket he got for speeding on a southern causeway. Aaron took him to the courthouse to pay the fine. We also noticed a dent on his back fender, of which he had no idea how it happened. It was time to discontinue driving.

April 27, 2021

We are fortunate that the big hurdle we faced (in our minds) of taking Justin's driving and truck away went as well as it did. It surprised us. We made an appointment with the dealership for routine service for his truck, with the secret plan to make up a story; there was a serious problem with the truck's engine. The engine had a crack in the block and couldn't be repaired. As the days went by (we left it at the dealership for them to sell), we had to repeat to Justin what was wrong many times, and eventually, he asked less and less about it.

During the next week, he also had an appointment with the family doctor, who told him it was time to quit diving for his and others' safety because of his FTD. (It was our plan with the doctor to tell him this.) This was the crisis point I thought would come, but it didn't! In the car later, he stated a few times that he was a careful driver, and I would agree, adding, "Gosh darn, that FTD," but then he'd forget, and we'd sing to the radio on the way home.

Over the next 20 days, we could eliminate the two dozen cookies he would eat every day because now he couldn't go to the grocery store and buy them. One of the harmful effects of FTD is the craving for sugar and carbs, of course, and they can't tell when they are full. Justin had gained almost 30 pounds, and the doctors always told him he needed to stop the sweets.

After that, one of us was always with him at the store. The cashier at our grocery store even mentioned as we went through her line, "No cookies today?" I told her, "No, he's eating healthier now!" He lost around 7 pounds, began riding his bike daily, and walked! His mood was up, and I could tell he felt better. (We do bring him a couple of healthy treats daily.)

Then something occurred to him. He could find someone who didn't know that he wasn't supposed to get those cookies! He could ask for a ride to the grocery store from the neighbors! He began his successful campaign and bought cookies again. He quit riding his bike and got more lethargic. I got mad at him and felt terrible because it wasn't his fault. He cannot help it.

Finally, he stopped asking for rides. We told the neighbors not to give him rides, too. He no longer gorges on cookies, feels better, and rides his bike again. It is incredible how reducing sugar makes him feel better. It's a lesson for us all!

One last thing: We are waiting for the completion of the facility he is eventually moving into, maybe in June. This is another big hurdle that hopefully won't be as big as we fear. He keeps bouncing back to his happy self, which makes us ever grateful. We are all determined to do what we can to foster his feeling of well-being.

I thank his excellent, kind doctors, Dr. H and Dr. J, for modern medicine and Ayurvedic practices that help him maintain his well-being. I'm grateful for our family, friends, and neighbors who help Justin know he is cared for and important. I also thank all the strangers who show such kindness and patience to Justin when he wants to show them something or tell them a story. It warms my heart.

April 31, 2021

It has been eventful since my last update. Justin is doing well, albeit with little shifts toward less competency and poorer short-term memory. He still smiles a lot. Childish impulses come and go.

What is new? I am still trying to figure out what happened to one of the garage door openers. Justin's brother, Aaron, removed everything from Justin's truck and found no opener.

We must assume Justin took it out before we took it in for the oil change (which became the end of the truck, with the damaged engine and crack in the block story). I mistakenly asked Justin where it might be, and then an idea got stuck in his brain that all the house keys were still in the truck! I shouldn't have brought it up.

He asked to be taken to his truck for about a week to retrieve the house keys. I showed him each time they were on the key hook in the kitchen, as always. Then he would argue that those are not the house keys, so we tried them. He was satisfied when they worked. Then, about 10 minutes later, we had to go through it again. And again. But he hadn't mentioned it in two days, so I crossed my fingers.

A caring neighbor noticed a strange man entering Justin's house on Saturday evening. She texted me a photo of his car and trailer. She said her 'mom radar' went up. Bill and I immediately went to Justin's house (3 minutes away), but the man had left. We asked Justin if he knew who he was, and he said he didn't know him, but he gave him some rosemary from his bush (Justin's way of making others happy, which is so who he has always been). Then, we discussed how he shouldn't let strangers in the house.

He told us he had the guy's name in his phone calendar, Steve, and he was coming back Sunday night at 7. Great. (Thank goodness Justin puts everything that happens on his phone so he can recall it.) On Sunday night, we were all at our house. When Justin wanted to go home before 7 for one of his favorite shows, my son, Aaron, followed him and waited for the guy. It turned out he was a neighbor living on the other side of Justin's circle.

The guy became nervous as Aaron explained the situation to him. Aaron also told him that the neighbors look out for Justin and that we ensure no funny business is happening. I think this neighbor is lonely. Who knows? But we are so grateful to Justin's other neighbor for contacting us. Thank you!

One of the scariest parts of him coming and going when and where he wants—if only on the bike now—is his interactions with strangers. As I have stated before, the challenge is trying to control a grown man who has little awareness that he isn't functioning logically, and we can't lock him up, for goodness' sake. Most assisted living facilities have a minimum age limit of 55. He is only 51 now.

But we are lucky that my representative at A Place for Mom guided me to a new facility 10 minutes away. It has independent living, assisted living, and memory care. We put a deposit down on a one-bedroom in independent living since he can mostly care for himself: shaving, doing laundry, fixing his breakfast, showering, etc.

He needs prompting for lunch and dinner and does not always recognize food choices. His taste has changed drastically, but with some tasting and encouragement, he usually eats well. He can go to the dining room for meals or bring them to his apartment at the new place. We will still stock his refrigerator there, too. Bill has generously handled this task. The dining room is a short walk from his door. And they will, or he may do his laundry. Housekeeping is included.

A great feature is that no one can come to see him unless they are on our approved list. He will be safe.

It has a beautiful courtyard with a coy pond, a workout area, a beauty/barber shop, a movie room, and a bistro/bar. Justin doesn't drink, so that won't be a problem!

Bill and I just went to the grand opening last Wednesday. We had a great time: fantastic food, live music, and the terrific staff. Bill won the big raffle prize! We also met the program director, who has 14 years of experience working with people with dementia. We stayed afterward and expressed our concerns to him: Justin's young age, no good place to bike ride, things to keep him busy, etc. The program director said he would go on bike rides with him! He will find out what Justin used to like to do, like wood shop things, and develop a program for him. He will be right beside him to 'work' on things. I also told him Justin loves to help people, and he said that's easy and he will have Justin help him with the older folks!!!

So, we are feeling hopeful that Justin will enjoy living there. Of course, I will continue to go daily to make sure he is taking his medicine and supplements and doesn't need anything.

I can see how trained staff can better handle someone with Justin's condition. Relatives are so emotionally involved. And sometimes, I lose patience. Saturday, he rode his bike over and sat and talked to me while I assembled Aaron's three-layer birthday cake. I turned my back, and he pulled out a big chunk of cake and shoved it in his mouth! I yelled at him. He looked so crushed that I felt awful. I hugged him and apologized, but it still goes into his internal, emotional storage. Very rough.

The facility is expected to obtain its certification and open sometime in June. Once the date is announced, we will begin the transition, planting seeds of a change in residence, figuring out how to explain it to him, and always assuring his comfort. Right now, the thought is telling him so much work has to be done on the house that he needs to stay in an apartment for a while.

His sense of time is off. He is so in the present moment. He thinks the truck was taken a week or two ago, and it's been two months. This is on our side.

On June 8, 2021, Justin was over at our house for dinner.

Kasey J. Claytor

June 15, 2021

My son has a form of early-onset dementia, so why is he so happy? Maybe it is only the stage he is at in this progressive disease. When I read or hear of others caring for those afflicted with this, they relate stories of bad behavior: lashing out, distrusting, berating family members, making exorbitant purchases, divorcing mates, etc.

It has been two years now since Justin was diagnosed. He showed signs a few years before, but they were so subtle that we didn't think anything about it. At the moment, my son is so happy that I feel almost guilty when I read others' stories. I haven't seen in any support groups anyone admit their loved one with FTD is happy. Maybe they see it like me. I am hesitant to talk about how well he is doing when others are suffering so much.

But on the other hand, maybe we are just doing something to foster his well-being. I can't say. It could be only how he is experiencing the illness. Everyone's path with this disease is unique, they say. If you know one person's symptoms with FTD, you only know one of many possibilities.

Again, FTD, or Frontotemporal Degeneration, is caused by shrinkage of the brain's frontal and/or temporal lobes. There is no known cause in modern medical research. The frontal lobe is responsible for problem-solving, executive functioning, short-term memory, social conditioning, etc. The temporal lobe is communication, language, remembering conversations, and aspects of visual perception.

Justin knows what he has. He seems to accept it. He is aware that his short-term memory is poor to non-existent. He has found a replacement for his poor memory. His phone. He has learned to brilliantly document all his day's activities in his phone calendar and add his plans to the schedule. I don't know how he does it because I can't find stuff on his phone that easily! He also takes a photo journal of all his medicines and supplements to ensure he doesn't take one twice, as well as his meals. When I came over to ask how his meal was, he quickly whipped out his phone and showed it to me, telling me how good it was.

He wasn't always this good at it. He used to get frustrated when he couldn't remember if he took a supplement and realized he may have taken it more than once or forgot to take the trash down the road. He used to try to hide his errors from us. But now he has moved into a place where he isn't embarrassed if he forgets; he goes to the phone.

He no longer forgets trash day, laundry day, or to shave, etc. He has gotten so easy to care for that I've let most of the caregivers go, and our family takes turns checking on him, stocking his fridge, taking him for outings, shopping, etc. He has his favorite shows, and if he is over at our house when one is coming on, he hops on his bike to go home.

Taking him out in public is becoming unpredictable. Sometimes, it's humorous, but it may also be a problem. I took him to a department store to buy him some underwear. A young woman on staff came up as we looked at the vast selection on the shelves. She asked, "What type of underwear are you looking for?"

Justin quickly unzipped and pulled down his jeans, declaring, "This kind!"

I pulled her aside later and explained what Justin had. There were lots of funny stories. It was like bringing a 6-foot-1-inch three-year-old with me, whom I had to watch closely. I do believe he listens to me better than he would listen to a spouse since he relates to me as his mother.

He was often in and out of our house since we lived nearby. He would come in and look for us. I was home alone one morning, upstairs, getting out of the shower. And here he comes bounding up the stairs to meet me face to face with me, buck naked! I hollered, "Justin!" and he, looking startled, turned and flew down the stairs!!!

Another time, he found me upstairs on the computer in my small office off the bedroom. I talked with him briefly and turned away to finish my email. When I came out, there he was with my old wig on and a big grin on his face.

He is continually expressing gratitude. He thanks all of us on a continuous thread, almost in every conversation.

He loves meeting people. He likes everyone. He will go up to anyone in the store and start singing, "It's a beautiful day in the neighborhood," or something like that. I often need to distract him from them to keep him from bothering people. But the other day, one woman began singing along with him! We winked at each other, bless her heart. He compliments people and says, 'Have a nice day!'.

I wonder where this happiness comes from. I mean, this is a serious, dire disease.

I wonder if our emphasis on an anti-inflammatory diet, herbs, herbal teas, and creating a calm environment as much as possible (inflammation is caused by emotions, too) has this effect. I love the intuitive sensibility of Ayurveda, an ancient healing tradition we integrate into our lifestyle. I lean toward believing yes.

But I think it is also his nature, now uncovered, released in all its loving glory. He was a self-conscious kid, half goofy joker and half shy. But he was always a seeker, reading and inquiring into our divine nature, God, and all creation. Of course, his self-consciousness is wholly gone because the part of his brain that tells him what is appropriate and culturally correct behavior is turned off.

Which makes him more like a child. A happy, grateful child. A Buddha boy.

I pray this lasts a long time and that I will never forget his happiness when it doesn't.

Kasey J. Claytor

July 3, 2021

We are moving closer to Justin's move-in date. The facility is finally opening, and the staff has been accommodating and comforting. They plan to keep him as busy as he wants (although FTD makes him tired quite a bit).

The move-in date is July 9, this Friday. We are all nervous about how it will go. He prefers to stay home, but I've already written about the safety issue of staying in a home where he isn't contained.

The staff is trained to help him be comfortable, and he is pretty easy to reassure.

His birthday was last week, and his cousin Krista flew in from California for a short visit. Justin was so excited, of course, and he called her the Best Cousin Ever! We hadn't seen her since COVID interrupted our lives.

Finding the Light

August 3, 2021

On July 9th, we moved Justin to the facility for his care and safety. To tell you it was hard is barely scratching the surface of my anguish. Logistically, we had it all worked out, and that part of the plan went as well as it could have. But you can't tell a heart to be logical, can you?

    I like to think that if we lived in a mature society and understood his childlike behavior and enthusiastic friendliness, Justin could have managed for a while longer without being moved. But we had to make this decision, even with the constant second-guessing of ourselves, before he found himself in a dangerous situation. The first few days were awful for all of us. But we got through it. He did need to move to memory care after a few days. It was too much for him in assisted living.

    He made friends right away. And every time I came to visit him, he told me all about them. And the good food!

After a week, he quit asking to go home. It has been three weeks now, and he is so comfortable. He regularly participates in activities (that we couldn't get him to do before), has people to socialize with whenever he wants, and tells me they clean his apartment and wash his clothes! I took him for a ride yesterday, a Starbucks drive-thru, and a short hike at a wildlife sanctuary. After about 100 feet into the park, he stopped, turned around, and said, "Ok, we can go back home now." And he meant his new 'apartment.'

He excitedly tells me there is a restaurant right down the hall where he eats sometimes, and he doesn't even have to order (making those decisions was hard for him). They bring him good food! And his supplements. He still documents everything on his phone so that I can check his pills, his food, and his shaving! LOL.

The residents are so well taken care of. The staff have been incredible, from the director to the program director and all the employees. The director is Justin's advocate. His stepmother had FTD, also. Justin is so young compared to the normal residents that they've had to adjust their customary service to meet Justin's needs. And my needs, I must say; they are so understanding and accommodating. They love Justin. Bill said he would be a star, and he is! We are so fortunate to have been led to this community. Thank you, my wonderful new friend, Terri, at *A Place for Mom*.

Visitation is currently limited because of the new delta variant in the COVID outbreak. Hopefully, those who are vaccinated will soon be able to see him. When you do, don't be surprised if, after 30 minutes or so, Justin says something like, "Well, I guess you'll be going soon, right?" Because he has things to do and people to meet!

We are beginning to relax now. It's a new reality. Tears still often gather behind my eyes, but I think we are all going to be OK.

Justin's name for me these past many months has been BME, Best Mom Ever. And I'm becoming known everywhere now as BME.

Kasey J. Claytor

I'm adding my rules for engaging with Justin below. Believe me, I need them.

10 Caregiving Rules
When Caring for Those with Dementia

If we can help them maintain a sense of well-being, that is the best measure of success.

1. Don't make them wrong
2. Don't argue
3. Re-direct, distract from unwanted activities
4. Compliment him/her often
5. Don't compare your loved one to his/her previous self; be open to how they are now and who they present.
6. Find things to appreciate about them now
7. Grieve who they were while not in their company
8. Graciously thank them for their offerings, even if you don't want what they offer!
9. Don't riddle them with questions or stop them from repeating a story. Usually, it's a story that gives them a sense of well-being to tell.
10. Celebrate the small or very small gifts—a smile, a task completed, unexpected successes

> re. #8 A neighbor of Justin's was helping, reporting to me Justin's activity while I wasn't there. He called me one day to tell me to please let Justin know that he does not want the rosemary Justin gave him from his

bush. He said he didn't like rosemary. One of Justin's pleasures was sharing his rosemary and his chicken's eggs. I wasn't about to tell him. This neighbor could have said thank you and just gotten rid of it.

At this time at his facility, it soon became obvious that many on the staff had no idea how to manage Justin and his compulsions.

August 31, 2021
To Staff at Justin's Memory Care

I understand the problem you are having with Justin taking sweets from other residents. Of course, that is unacceptable. I just had a conversation with my theaftd.org counselor, who told me this is, unfortunately, common with FTD patients. The part of their brain that monitors right from wrong is dying. What is left is the amygdala, the part that seeks pleasure like that rush from sugar. Unlike other common dementias, he has the behavioral variant of FTD. You can't change it, but you can work around it. Different experts have told me that psychological talk therapy isn't appropriate for FTD patients either. They can't change and don't remember what was said.

Physically, he is in good shape and has a lot of energy. He was driving up until about six months ago, and he would drive to the store every day and buy a big box of cookies. My always-thin son gained almost 30 pounds. We had no control over it until we took his truck away. Then something miraculous happened. He got off sugar with us giving him low glycemic treats, bananas, and nuts for snacks. Then, he began riding his bike every day, and he lost all that weight. We could tell he felt good. He quit asking for sweets.

So, it is possible, but now we realize the other residents have those items within Justin's reach. It isn't fair to them to have to change the way they keep their treats.

I am still optimistic that the staff can handle taking care of this. I see three possibilities:

1. Considering his energy, I see a guy who needs exercise. It's calming, tires him out, and is good for his brain, among many other benefits. Maybe show him how to use the equipment in the exercise room or allow him to ride his bike that is stored there.
2. Justin has a neurology appointment in early November, and we will see if the Doc has any suggestions. (It would be sad to drug him so he isn't a problem and sits, staring. The time will come in the disease that he will lose all interest in anything soon enough)
3. We take him home and hire someone to be a companion/caregiver or move him to the Traumatic Brain Injury facility on Merritt Island.

Also, I might suggest looking up Teepa Snow on YouTube. She has a large number of videos on how to handle such situations. She is amazing.

Sandi Lutz, a support leader for the AFTD organization, is available to speak with the staff about helpful ideas for FTD individuals. Let me know when/if there is a good time.

A great 15-minute **60 Minutes** piece on FTD is on YouTube.

I believe this can be solved through distraction, redirecting, keeping him busy, and using the resourcefulness of your excellent staff. It is temporary.

Warm Regards,
Kasey Claytor, BME

> The following is from my notes: One of my biggest causes of pain was knowing some staff at Justin's facility would make him feel bad because of their responses and beliefs about him. I am learning now that this is something I can never control, so getting upset about it only hurts me. I have to believe his experience is not my responsibility. It's his and God's. It's a hard lesson.
>
> And: I hate that I'm becoming familiar with Western medical terms.
>
> Another aside. How do you rectify his accomplishment of buying and paying off his home now with his inability to live in it? The enjoyment of his land, plants, fruit trees, and hobbies of surfing, kayaking, fishing, and motorcycle riding, with his now single room, fake grass outside, with doors that stay shut to him?
>
> After we moved Justin out of his house, I found another journal he had kept for months. Words in

Thai he had learned from his wife were sprinkled throughout. He was staying so positive. We were just amazed. I'm sure he did it because he knew he was forgetful. In each entry, he greeted the day and told of the nice walks with the dog, the good meals he had, the tasks completed, how many eggs the chickens laid, and what bills he paid.

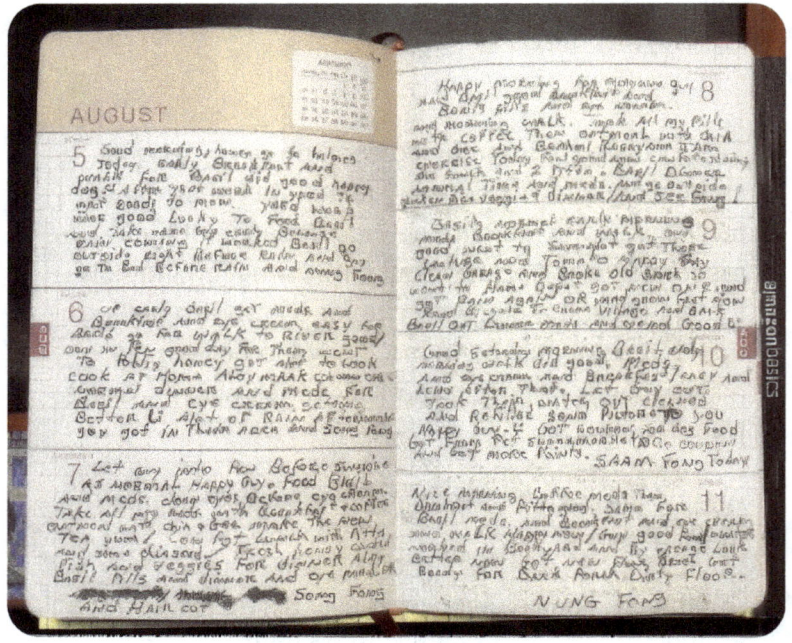

September 23, 2021

I am back from a retreat, rested and ready to work and handle all that matters for Justin. Unfortunately, he is progressing, causing more problems for other residents and staff. His craving for food, especially sweets, drives him to look everywhere for 'snacks.' On top of that, he is very friendly with residents and their guests, getting in their personal space and affectionately patting them!

The staff continues to complain to me, so we are trying a different medication and having the support person from theaftd.org speak to the staff via Zoom. (Only one plus the director signed up to attend, though!)

Aaron discovered that Justin loves playing catch with a toy football! I found a beach ball in his room, and we tossed that back and forth, too. He grinned the whole time.

Thank you to all who have taken the time to visit him! He loves the attention and shows me pictures of the visits. You are all so kind. In addition, someone from Justin's old company is visiting him soon. He will be so surprised. He may need a little reminding of who those visiting are, but usually, giving him some time, he will remember.

During his stay in this brand-new facility, most of the staff are Certified Nursing Assistants. Most are caring and mean well. I don't add this to frighten you; I only want to make you aware of the deficit in the training of CNAs for memory care facilities, in my opinion. We are located in Florida, and the hours to attain a CNA certification is 120, equivalent to 15 days. Therefore, the specialty of handling residents with dementia is left up to the memory care units. There is no way you can cover the focused care of these diverse residents in that amount of time. I have observed that it takes more training, maturity, patience, and understanding. It has become apparent that it is a big ask, considering our experience.

I received a call asking me to talk with Justin and tell him to quit coming into the nurse's station. Many times, when I came in to see him, I was told to please tell him not to do this or that. He has no short-term memory. What are they thinking?

I also received a call at 11:00 PM telling me Justin had broken into the freezer and had taken some ice cream. What am I supposed to do about it? (The freezer was chained with a padlock. We were pretty amazed he figured out how to get into it!) These are a few examples. (More is in the letter I wrote to the CEO of the parent company, which I've included.)

My counselor, Sandi, affiliated with the tremendous resource—The Association for Frontotemporal Degeneration (theaftd.org)—told me a story. He wore a woman's bracelet when she visited her husband in memory care. Of course, she immediately knew he had taken it from someone's room. She brought him to the nurse's station to find out where it belonged. The nurse was brilliant.

She said, "Why, that is such a nice bracelet! Oh my, may I wear it for a few minutes?" He happily handed it to her. Now, if they had admonished him and demanded that he hand it over, he would probably have balked and felt attacked, holding onto it tightly. From his perspective, it was his because it was on his wrist. He quickly forgot it ever existed by giving it voluntarily and walking away. This works almost all the time. Their short-term memory is usually non-existent.

Finding the Light

Sharing from a person with dementia who found this online:

"Boundaries are an executive function. That's one of the first things to go with SOME cases of dementia. This makes disciplining someone with dementia even more challenging. NOT impossible. The logic concept simply doesn't exist. Dementia Symptoms and Executive Functioning: Dementia symptoms related to impairment of executive functioning, involve the ability to think abstractly, plan, initiate and carry out complex behavior. On mental status examination, individuals with these dementia symptoms display problems coping with new tasks. Interestingly, although memory impairment often goes along with executive impairment, a person can show no memory problems but still be impaired in decision-making and executive functioning. On a practical level, impairments in executive functioning have been associated with impairments in activities of daily living which include getting dressed, the ability to feed oneself, bathe oneself and more. Executive functioning ability has been strongly connected to working memory ability. Other examples of impaired executive functioning in dementia include poor judgment, disorganization, socially inappropriate behavior, difficulty making plans for an event later in the day, and an inability to understand how their behavior or choices affect those around them. Executive functioning impairments may make it seem like the person is behaving selfishly, especially if their memory is still quite intact."

–James Hamilton, Cdp, www.seniorcarepsychological.com

Kasey J. Claytor

November 7, 2021

Justin is mostly thrilled with visitors, but sometimes, he wants to be left to himself or with the other residents and staff. Perhaps it's because I fuss over the room and clean up the messes, but sometimes, he is tired. I've heard from other FTDers that it is exhausting trying to remember things, answer questions, be correct, make the right decisions, etc. Then I remember my friend Brent, a psychotherapist and Vedic astrologer (interesting combo), who says it is most important to be present. Listen when he wants to talk. Enjoy their company. Enjoy their 50th telling of a story.

He is always ready for a ride, albeit shorter than he used to like. He's become a homebody. When I walk into his room, the first thing he always says now is, "Hi, Mom! Can we go for a ride?"

There hasn't been much to report, so you haven't heard from me for a while. Family members visit almost daily, and his cousin came to see him when she visited from California. He likes it and is happy where he is. He knows when we are driving and getting close to his 'apartment building.'

I took him to a new neurologist, thinking I'd like a different perspective on his medication. The doctor will let me know in a week or so. It is getting hard for me to take him alone because he is all over the place, going for any food items or new people, having no personal boundaries, etc. Because of COVID rules, only one companion may accompany the patient.

Finding the Light

Aaron took a video of Justin playing the piano at his facility. He played a little piece I taught him when he was a child. It's interesting what parts of the brain remain untouched: where he is in space, directions, childhood memories, and people from long ago. He told me about a place we lived when he was so small yesterday; I couldn't believe it.

> The new neurologist I took Justin to seemed a bit odd to me. He questioned why I was bringing him in, even though I told him I wanted him to evaluate Justin's medications. After talking for about 20 minutes, he said he would call me with his opinion, but he never did! That was the last time I took Justin by myself. He was zooming all over the building, and he was very hard for me to control.

December 30, 2021

We have been lying low from communicating with all of you because we were blindsided by the news that we were told Justin had to leave the place he loved so much. There is a lot to the story; they dumbfounded me with the complaints about him that amounted to nothing unusual for a person with dementia. The director with knowledge of FTD left and was replaced by someone with *no hands-on experience with dementia patients.*

The bad news is that hurriedly finding a place for him, especially during the holidays, was extremely difficult.

Prejudice in the memory care community against younger dementia patients is commonplace.

This hit at the same time we lost a family member, one of Bill's brothers. Not to mention, work is demanding, though it is a good diversion for me and something I enjoy.

The good news! Justin moved into a new facility yesterday and has already adjusted; actually, he did immediately. They adore him, and he adores all of the staff. They have all come up to me astonished that he was made to leave the other place; he is so easy and happy. (And safe!) And continues to tell us how the food is great, healthy, and free!

I told him he had to change apartments because his old one was too small. I believe he thinks he is in the same place but in a different building, five minutes from the other place. He is right at home and doesn't want to leave it for long. (Dear friends said some powerful prayers. I prayed and meditated three or more times a day.)

I've reprinted here the letter I sent to the company's CEO that kicked Justin out. He responded that he was sorry and would look into it. The staff has low morale, and two who had great affection for Justin have now left.

MESS WITH ME? I'LL LET KARMA DO ITS JOB. MESS WITH MY FAMILY? I BECOME KARMA.

Finding the Light

Justin's New Apartment

Here is the letter I sent:
Dear Mr. ____,

When we moved our son, Justin Wade, into one of your facilities, we had confidence in the team, admired the director very much, and connected well with your marketing representative. Justin had a rough start but finally settled well in memory care. Most caregivers developed a good relationship with him, and he's enjoyed living there so much that he doesn't want to be away from it for long. He is always cheerful and loves everyone.

But I started getting calls that seemed strange to me because your staff was calling me at night and at work to tell me Justin was wandering into other residents' rooms. Justin was taking items from other's rooms. Justin figured out how to get ice cream from the locked freezer (this call was at 11 at night!). Justin, craving carbs and sugar, was searching for stuff to eat or picking up pretty, attractive things. (I found out later the reason they crave sweets is because they lose the ability to taste other tastes.) I would tell them, yes, that is dementia.

What I learned from research and interviews with other facilities' directors:

1. Wandering halls and going into rooms is common among dementia patients. They view all the area they live in as their home and do not see boundaries.
2. They will pick up items from around the facility and take them to their room. Dementia experts call this 'shopping'.
3. We can't change their behavior, so we change their environment.

On his second day, the new director called about Justin entering a room where the resident had visitors. The director acted like Justin had committed a terrible crime. He also said Justin opened the resident's closed door, which is impossible because the doors automatically lock.

As I toured other facilities to find a new home for him, several residents flowed in and out of the resident's rooms we were in. No one was alarmed. And they were cheerful to the wanderer, helping them with whatever they needed.

My son is like a 6-foot toddler, and when he wants something strongly, he will, though rarely, tug on my sleeve, as a child does. He did this to one of the people in charge because this person kept a big bowl of candy in plain sight. Justin can't shut off his desire for candy when he sees it. He was told no and then tugged on this person's sleeve. (I had asked for this bowl to be put out of sight. Then there is no problem.) But this person got unnerved and thought Justin was becoming aggressive. (He is not)

The truth is that a minority of FTD dementia patients do go through an aggressive phase. But we've never seen it with Justin. We are with him several times a week. I've asked the caregivers who are with him daily, and they've never seen it.

However, that experience with that person was enough for this new director to tell me swiftly and abruptly that Justin was no longer wanted there. I think the person who complained read something about Justin's illness and became frightened with worries and what-ifs.

This new director also said it looked bad for people coming in to look at the facility and see a 'younger' dementia resident!

This is why I had to set upon a hurried search for another facility and learn all about the behaviors of other dementia residents. Some of the facilities sent over their experts to talk with Justin and interview the caregivers individually, and they were perplexed as to why he was getting kicked out. Everyone they spoke to said Justin has no problematic behaviors, he is a joy, and they all love him. They told me this, too, and were surprised he was being told to leave. I won't even go into how this has affected our family. It is beyond hurt.

We are excited about Justin's new living arrangements. We have hopefully found a place where he is welcomed, where he doesn't have doors slammed in his face or hear a raised voice telling him "No!". (And he looks down. It breaks my heart. Our whole family has seen this.)

I wanted to let you know about the shortfalls within your facility. Most employees are trying their best and doing well; I respect and admire them. They are doing what we cannot do, and we appreciate it enormously.

I do think ongoing education and staff training will correct this. Prospective employees should be fielded for prejudice against those whose behaviors cannot be helped. Also, other residents' families should be educated on what they might observe in memory care.

A head nurse at another place told me the men in memory care were urinating on plastic plants in their hall. She said you can't change their behavior, so she removed the plants. Problem solved. Another facility locks up personal possessions, toiletries, etc., in their room's cupboard and will open it for the resident when needed, but it stops the 'shopping.'

I wanted to do your survey, but I think someone has already removed Justin from the system; I can't access it through the website, though I keep getting requests to do so.

Finding the Light

Justin is moving out on December 29. Many caregivers want to visit him in his new place, which says a whole lot to us.

Peace and Happy New Year.
Sincerely,
Kasey Claytor

> The new director was a large man who previously worked in accounting, which explained his lack of knowledge. He told me that Justin asked him for a snack, and when he said 'no,' Justin pulled on his lapel. The director commented, "And me being the size I am!" as if that would matter to Justin. It didn't register. Shortly after my letter, I learned that this new director was fired.

Chapter 4: 2022

February 7, 2022

All is exceptionally well! January 29th marked one month in Justin's new place. It was a lot of work behind the scenes for me, my husband, Bill, and Aaron. From Justin's perspective, he went for a long ride and returned to his 'apartment.' It was set up just like his old one as much as possible. He continues to be happy and so easygoing. The bit of hurt and frustration he showed at the previous place is completely gone. This new facility is solely memory care.

The typical dementia behaviors are now taken in stride with knowing smiles and loving patience. I was surprised to discover they adhere to the Montessori caregiving method in their staff training. And I thought that was just for children! But it makes perfect sense because it allows the resident's self-determination and choices, keeping their dignity.

(The previous facility had little to no memory care training, and since he is young, they kept trying to 'teach' him to stop behaviors beyond his control, like walking in through open doors.)

Where he is now, they listen politely as he tells them about his family for the umpteenth time. They all show genuine warmth and acceptance toward him. They never complain to me about his behavior like the previous place had. Some asked me what the problem was in the last place. When I tell them, they tell me they adore him and cannot believe what the previous director told me. We can't either. But it is such a blessing that he was made to leave because I would have never found the place he is in now.

I learned that some fine workers from the previous place have left because of the hard-line management of the memory care unit.

Anyway, I have been advised to let the past go for my emotional health! So, I will try not to bring it up anymore.

We take Justin for rides several times a week. He loves riding in the car. We turn the radio up and sing to his old favorites. We may buy a snack at Starbucks. He waves at everyone, especially truck drivers! We ride down the river road, and he waves at all the walkers. If they wave back, he is beside himself with happiness. "Did you see? She waved back at me!"

I pray he continues like this. If you are down, you need to hang out with Justin, and you cannot be anything but happy!

> I contacted St. Francis Hospice about this time, and a nice gentleman came to interview Justin and me. Justin didn't qualify for Hospice assistance. He was too mobile, I think, even though he was terminal. So, I would wait until he progressed more down the road. However, we hired a St. Francis nurse practitioner, later on, someone anyone can hire, and she was invaluable in assessing his medication.

April 25, 2022

Justin is making his family famous in his new digs! When we walk in, we are BME and BBEs: Best Mom Ever, Best Brother Ever, and Best Bill Ever. Yesterday, as I walked with Justin through the halls, two gentlemen visiting relatives there came up to me and said, you must be Kasey, BME! They learn we live on the river and what cars we drive! (Because Justin tells everyone!)

Justin only vaguely remembers that we have been there all the times we go to see him. This makes one understand that it isn't the outside recognition of us doing the right thing that we do; it's the inner knowing that we have. Having a family member like this is an extremely long and deep lesson. A lesson no one wants, but once in it, one knows the value.

When I was younger, I used to get offended when people felt sorry for me. My take was that they thought I wasn't up to handling it. Now, when someone expresses sympathy, I understand they're just being with me and my situation, feeling into my experience, and I appreciate it. It's especially hard for others who haven't been through something like this to comprehend it.

It's not the crises and traumas that fuel our growth; it is the self-inquiry and inner work done to heal from them.

I also believe we have a reservoir inside that contains our feelings of grief, sadness, and well-being. The more kindness those around Justin show him, making him feel seen and important, the more his reservoir fills with good feelings and a sense of well-being. This is of utmost importance now.

I often tell people that no matter what is going on in my life or how busy I am, when I am with Justin, all that disappears, and I am present with him. Consequently, spending time with him is a big lift for me. It is truly a moment out of time. It's counterintuitive and something I would have never imagined. He is so innocent.

I had lunch with the executive director of the facility Justin is in now. She kept telling me how much he was loved there. He is always happy. When she gives a tour to a new family, he will often tag along and tell them how good and healthy the food is and what a nice day it is here. The director said, "He is like our best advocate!"

I routinely check his phone and clean out the spam he gets. Lately, he has been getting many texts asking if he is interested in selling his house. He always texts back, "No, but it is a really nice day here. There is a good restaurant near my apartment, and the food is healthy and free!" They never text again! We get a good chuckle at that.

However, he is increasingly unable to use the phone correctly. I often run it down to the shop because something has gone wrong. I am afraid he won't be able to manage it much longer. I text him daily and often don't get a response, but he usually answers a phone call.

Lastly, I copied a post my dear friend and fellow author, Donna Miesbach, wrote to her subscribers. She gets it.

"Dear Ones All,

A dear friend of mine has an adult son who incurred serious brain damage, which took away all of his biases, opinions, and, yes, his plans. You may be wondering what could possibly be left. Well, what was left was a radiant, unbounded, over-the-top love for all people, no matter who they are. He sees everyone as they truly are – beautiful.

Because of his limitations, he is now in a care facility, but he is so happy. He is like a light shining in darkness. Even though his life has changed significantly, he is showing us what we, too, can be like when all of our biases and opinions are gone.

Initially, this must have seemed like such a terrible loss to his family, but in God's economy, nothing is ever wasted. God is using this young man to show us what pure love is like.

In losing just about everything, her son was left with what mattered the most.

It makes me wonder what our lives – and our world – would be like if we could let go of our biases and opinions, too.

Something to think about, wouldn't you say…

Sending you love,

Donna Miesbach"

July 16, 2022

It has been a while since I last wrote about Justin (April). Not a whole lot has changed, but of course, there are the little things that are constantly changing. Justin is still happy, friendly, and totally in the moment. I am still uplifted whenever I visit him. He remembers most of us all the time and needs his memory refreshed for others.

He caught COVID, and we had to stop seeing him for a week. He only had a raspy voice and a slight cough and was tired. He breezed right through it and insisted he was fine! Our doctor prescribed a new anti-viral drug and a mild sedative to keep him from running around, exposing everyone, while he was supposed to be quarantined. The executive director had tried to find a COVID bed in a nursing facility for him, but no beds were available. I think that would have been quite disastrous because he is so hard to control. He knows the routine there, and we worked on ideas to keep him in his room and use a mask. I spoke to the FTD counselor, and she suggested when he asks to take a walk, take him on a short one in an empty hall and then right back to his room for a little treat. When we talked to him on the phone, we told him to stay in his room so no one could catch his " flu. "

We made it through that, but I have no idea where he caught it.

Justin's compulsion to eat anything and everything is still present and of concern. It is typical of the stage he is at. I took small candies down for staff to 'trade' with him when he took a big cookie or a pudding cup. He will easily take a substitute. We are all so grateful he is there. They are so compassionate and understanding. And they listen to our ideas and suggestions as we listen to theirs. We all have the same goal: to give him the best care possible.

He is becoming less aware of his self-care; however, things like brushing his teeth, putting dirty clothes in the hamper, putting clean clothes on, etc., need prompting. A few weeks ago, he had two accidents, so he transitioned to pullups, but as far as I know, there have been no accidents since then.

We have two sides of ourselves: our egoic side, anchored in the material world, and our spiritual side, linked to our higher self, intuition, creativity, and God. When I am in my ego, I hold the reality of Justin's tragic situation, as well as that of our whole family, and the depressing understanding that his condition will degrade. His future is not what he or anyone wanted for him, and it will be tough to watch.

On the spiritual side, knowing the deeper currents running under our existence, there is so much more. I have been calling Justin my little Buddha boy. He is always innocent in the present, without judgment, joyful, without worry, and filled with gratitude. How in the world can this be? In all of my research, I've not come across anyone with his diagnosis who would be described this way. One of life's mysteries? Or not.

"Oh, give me the beat, boys, and free my soul
I wanna get lost in your rock 'n' roll and drift away"

Morning Ride

We float down the road
On our morning ride

Drift Away begins to play
Immediately
Justin begins to sing

And I hear the words
"And when my mind is free"
I know
his is
in this moment

Something happens inside me
joy rises within
As I look at him
Lost in your rock'n'roll
And in his presence
Is peace

Drift Away by Williams, Mentor R
Sung by Dobie Gray

    I usually put on the Yacht Rock radio station for Justin while on our rides. They play mostly 80s and 90s easy rock: Michael McDonald, Kenny Loggins, The Doobie Brothers, Christopher Cross, Steely Dan, etc. In many songs, Justin still remembers the words and happily sings along. It makes him so happy.

    While searching online for a good birthday gift for him, I found a 'radio' for dementia patients. It is a large box with a big on/off switch and volume dial. It is a simple music player/MP3. It is easy to operate. I loaded several songs from the playlist of his favorite station—all the songs we sing to! He plays it often. Sometimes, when I come into his room, he is in his bed listening to it.

Also, I bought him a digital frame this year, and we loaded it with many family photos. The neatest thing is that when we come across a photo that we think he'd like, we can send it to his device with an app on our phones. He often sits and contentedly watches as the pictures float by.

Brotherly Van Rides

Aaron closes our office at noon every Friday. We run a financial advisory firm. Each Friday afternoon, Aaron would take his old 1985 VW Vanagon and drive 30 miles to visit Justin and give him a ride. Justin loved the van. Occasionally, I would be at the facility at the same time.

One afternoon, I decided to ride with them. I hopped into the van and sat on the broad backseat. There were my two boys: Aaron driving and Justin in the passenger seat. Aaron was very attentive, listening to Justin and pointing out things Justin would like. Kindness is an understatement. The brotherly love was palpable.

Then, before Aaron needed to shift to the next gear, he told Justin, "Put it in second, Justin." Justin grinned and, with ease, moved the old floor gears from muscle memory. This continued as I sat in the back with tears running down my face, in utter awe and gratitude.

July 18, 2022

Looking back at my earliest writings about Justin's FTD, I came across two mentions of Justin's 'repressed anger' from experts I consulted with. I had forgotten about that. How do I rectify this with the apparent contentment and joy he exudes now?

First, he isn't capable of withholding the expression of his emotions any longer. He doesn't have the higher adult functioning that would enable him to hide any emotional response. Like a toddler who expresses whatever they are feeling, he shows mostly joy but occasional, short-lived frustration. And it is almost always concerning food due to his compulsion. Yet, he is appeased relatively easily.

So, if this was true, where did this repressed anger (according to Ayurveda, leading to inflammation) that could be causing his brain shrinkage come from? We took care of him for two years and gave him Ayurvedic supplements, teas, and mostly vegetarian food. We kept him in the best situation possible for his comfort and ease. Now, he's in a facility that mostly continues the supplements, but the diet isn't conducive to reducing inflammation.

Yet he appears to have no underlying anger. If there had indeed been some stored anger, it would have shown itself by now.

> For those caring for someone with FTD, be prepared to hear 'No' a lot. Reminiscent of toddlerhood, Justin would declare his aversion to something with a simple NO. I imagine it is harder for a spouse or adult child caregiver than a parent, for in the deep recesses of our memories of their childhood, it comes up as familiar and doesn't cause a strong reaction in us.

August 7, 2022

Dear *(A new facility director, again!),*
I got a phone call from a staff member on Justin's phone wanting me to tell Justin to stop taking other residents' food. She didn't hear about the candy switch. She thought he was hungry, and they'd given him pudding and cookies. They argued with him about taking other people's food, which doesn't help. She said he pushed someone. I don't blame the staff because they probably have not been told how to handle this.

I told her to have the nurse give her some of the candies and tell Justin she has a treat for him if she sees him going for other people's food or asking for a snack. I told all of the staff I could, but many still don't know this.

We are all exasperated. I told her he wasn't hungry and that giving him sugary snacks would not make any difference.

The new marketing director told me it would be great to let the new wellness director know. I'd like a conference with all the directors. I met her a week ago, and she said they would eventually get around to it and that they had to have a meeting like that with every resident's family. I guess it will be a long way away.

Please tell the staff and the CNAs Justin has no control over his obsession with food. That part of the brain is dying. They need to be smart and trick him into taking a substitute treat. I can tell him a hundred times a day, but that won't do anything but hurt him.

This article was in the Neurology Today:

"*A new study found atrophy in the ventral insula, striatum, and anterior orbitofrontal cortex among overeating patients with frontotemporal dementia.

A disease that robs a person of lifetime identity also claims a hold on appetite, leaving patients with frontotemporal dementia victim to overeating and even death by food consumption.

Now, the University of California-San Francisco (UCSF) investigators who put frontotemporal dementia on the diagnostic map have pinpointed the brain region damaged in these binge-eaters

Bruce L. Miller, MD, and his colleagues at UCSF had witnessed enough bizarre and uncontrolled consumption of food in patients with frontotemporal dementia that they set out to identify the brain regions that could explain the ravenous eating behavior. The patients seem to have normal taste recognition, and they can report when they feel full, but none of that gets in the way of their propensity to gorge on food.

Dr. Miller, who led the study, is a professor of neurology at UCSF, where he holds the AW & Margaret Clausen Distinguished Chair. He is also the clinical director of the UCSF Memory and Aging Center.

LOSS OF BRAIN TISSUE IN OVEREATERS

The UCSF team used MR voxel-based morphometry to study 32 patients with neurodegenerative disease and 18 healthy controls. They discovered that six of the patients who continued to eat way beyond satiety all had a loss of brain tissue in the ventral insula, striatum, and orbitofrontal cortex. All six had been diagnosed with frontotemporal dementia.

Other studies have pinpointed these same circuits in case reports of extreme overeaters with obsessive-compulsive disorder and bulimia. But this is the first time that scientists have set out to find the source of overeating in patients with this mind-robbing, personality-altering condition.

In defining damaged systems in these patients, the scientists believe that they have identified the regions that govern feeding and food choice. "Satiety is not sufficient to suppress eating," the scientists wrote. "Patients with atrophy of this circuit continue to perceive satiety but fail to translate satiety signals into appropriate action plans."

Let me know what I can do to help.
Kasey Claytor, AKA BME

August 20, 2022

I am now aware of why they call dementia the long goodbye. Little by little, Justin is slowly withdrawing from the goings-on around him. He no longer follows the news (not bad), his favorite shows, others outside his primary family, and anything out of his immediate environment.

Remember when your kids were about one or two years old, and the concept of mine and yours hadn't crystalized yet? And they would grab what they wanted and declare "mine!" Even the lines of "your room and my room" are blurred. Their frontal lobe, with that reasoning ability, hadn't developed yet. Justin is in rewind. With his frontal lobe diminishing, those around him find it necessary to continue shifting his care plan.

I watch him trying to understand why he shouldn't take that drink sitting by another's plate or why he can't have something. He can't grasp it anymore, and sometimes, he gets frustrated by those around him. They don't understand; all this is his! The whole building he is in is his home. All the contents are his, of course.

It causes me to wonder when, in our evolution, we began carving up 'things' into mine and yours. And will we ever return to a way of being before that; is it a higher way of being? Recall John Lennon's lyrics in *Imagine*,

> Imagine no possessions
> I wonder if you can
> No need for greed or hunger
> A brotherhood of man
>
> Imagine all the people
> Sharing all the world

Because of his irritation with being told it isn't his while putting a vise grip on it, or being told he can't do that, or he must do this, we've found it necessary to increase his medication. It slows him a bit and doesn't change his perception, but he's not as cranky, and redirecting him is a bit easier.

Justin still tells me he loves me, so I taught him the little song "I love you, a bushel and a peck, a bushel and a peck, and a hug around the neck, hug around the neck." (Remember Doris Day?) "A Bushel and a Peck" is a popular song by Frank Loesser, published in 1950.

I took Justin for a ride recently, and he sang it to me several times between our singing to the radio. One of the nurses said he came up to her the other day and sang it to her!

His most commonly uttered words are 'thank you,' still. He often remains in gratitude.

We take one day at a time. It isn't easy, but at the same time, eye-opening into a different world.

Response to this last Justin update
From Donna Miesbach

Dear, dear Kasey,

From what you are telling us, it sounds (to me) like he is returning to his original state of consciousness where there are no divisions. The ocean and the wave concept come to mind. It's all the ocean, but we don't see that when we are focused so intently on being the wave.

There is great peace in the oneness. Nothing is wrong; nothing needs to be fixed, and nothing needs to be done because everything is already perfect, just the way it is.

Now that his "anchor" is settling into that blissful state, the memories of the divisions we live with every day are evaporating. For those of us who are still dealing with divisions, it would be difficult trying to get him to fit into our ways of doing things. This doesn't make how we do things wrong. It's just that the frequency we are on is different, and different "rules" apply.

So yes, the transition is difficult for you and him. What you are asking him to do doesn't fit the paradigm he is harkening to now.

Please be patient with yourself, just as you already are with him. He is opening up to a realm we cannot yet see, but it is real.

Sending you much, much love, Kasey. You are all in my thoughts and prayers.

–Donna

September 15, 2022
To the Current Facility Director

Every piece of negative news about my son *feels like* a stab in my heart, with no balancing reassurance and no possible positive outcome. The pain is impossible to quantify.

I know you are doing your best and protecting your charges. I wholeheartedly support you.

My perspective, of course, is different from that of caregivers.

I see him lying on his bedspread, sleeping in his clothes, the cold air blowing on him all night. The blue and tan quilt he used to sleep under keeps getting misplaced. He doesn't comprehend he can sleep under any other covers. He did this at home, too.

He thinks he showered and brushed his teeth because he always used to, but he doesn't realize he forgot to.

He is taking off the depends because they are heavy and wet, but he doesn't understand that he needs to wash up and put on another pair. When I come in, he has nothing under his pants.

His compulsiveness with eating is not driven by hunger. His satiation response doesn't cause him to stop eating. Caregivers, thinking he is hungry, give him second breakfasts, many snacks, and multiple sugary drinks, thinking that will satisfy him when a small piece of candy will do. Giving in to his compulsion, he would eat himself to death. I would not know this if it weren't for seeing it when I was there or him calling one of us and telling us what was happening right then. "Oh, they are bringing me two glasses of juice!" At 9:00 am, after he had eaten breakfast earlier, he said, "I asked for breakfast, and they are giving me a plate right now! Thank you," etc.

One of our comforts is his ability to call and text us. When he does, we are reassured that he is OK. It has been a gift and a lifeline that we knew would eventually come to an end. But we could never be prepared for it—that loss of connection.

For the last three years, he has taken pictures of who he talked to, what he ate, and where he went in the car as a replacement for his frontal lobe to remember what he did and who he spoke to.

The staff's use of fear to control Justin is deeply hurtful. It demonstrates a lack of training and maturity. They tell him what they want him to do or stop doing and say, "I will call your mom." I'd never thought staff would do this.

There is a book by Oliver James called *Contented Dementia*. It is an excellent book with ideas and perspectives on caring for dementia patients. In it, he eloquently explains how, even though the mental faculties aren't 100% anymore, their emotional self and sense of well-being are still felt 100%. All emotions are still there. Unlike information, which is lost or evaporates, feelings are stored within. Consequently, if the sufferer is in situations that cause fear or anger often, it decreases their sense of well-being. It can affect their whole daily experience.

No one is purposely doing a poor job. Everyone, including Justin, is doing the best they can.

Most will view Justin as this big man acting strangely and seemingly capable of understanding, but those who love him understand he has no choice in acting and reacting, incapable of control. We still see who he is inside, his innocent soul. He was always ready to help any relative, friend, or co-worker.

Your leadership in this issue is integral to Justin's well-being. I thank you for being focused and invested in a good outcome.

–Kasey Claytor

November 21, 2022
To Caregivers

You are doing an amazing job, and I admire you. Few people could do it, and you come in every day ready to care for our family members.

I want to make it easier on you, if at all possible. After four years of Justin's condition, I've learned some things that may be helpful to you.

Justin's frontal lobe is dying. That part of the brain is where adult behavior, impulse control, problem-solving, and comprehension functions. This means:

1. He will often not understand questions, especially long ones.
2. He won't understand requests involving several steps, such as sitting down, taking your shoes off, and getting undressed. It's too much to grasp.
3. If he doesn't understand and someone tries to make him 'obey' them, he will automatically say NO because he doesn't get it.
4. He will not remember something in a few minutes if he is told something. He has no short-term memory. Occasionally, something that is repeated many, many times will make it into his long-term memory.
5. He will be frightened and balk if he is grabbed or moved without someone telling him what they are doing and why.
6. If he is told no, it isn't productive; he will disagree because he doesn't understand what is happening.
7. He is losing his sense of taste, the ability to tell what is edible, and the ability to sense when he is full. Therefore, he eats as much as is available.

Things that do work *most* of the time:

8. Avoid using the word No. Find creative ways to make him right. If he grabs something that is not his, "Oh Justin, you found my _____. Thank you

so much!" Or, "That is so nice. May I borrow it for a little while?"
9. Compliment him often. Let him hear, "That's right, Justin!" "You're so smart!" "Right!!!" You are filling him with a sense of well-being, which dementia patients can still experience.
10. Justin's thinking is vastly impaired, yet his emotional life is intact. He feels the same emotions we do. We are responsible for creating the experience that will give him a sense of well-being.
11. We all use re-direction. It can be in a fun-loving way with a big smile. "Justin, I have something special for you over here!" No matter how often you use it, it will be new to him.
12. Use humor. Tell him when/if you screw up, apologize. These make him feel good.
13. Ask him for help. "Will you help me move this chair?" He loves to be helpful, giving him a sense of purpose. He was helpful to everyone he met his whole life. He was the first to stop and help someone on the side of the road, fill up the tires on his co-worker's car, help with their projects, help family members with big jobs around our homes, etc.
14. Battering him with questions makes him feel stupid and confused. Talk around the topic, "It is a good time for a shower now, and later, you can have a snack." Instead of, "Don't you need to get in the shower now?" You'll hear a no. He may not even comprehend, 'shower.'.

15. I screw up all the time. Please don't think I have this all down myself. We are all trying!
16. Be present with him. Observe him. Try to figure out what he wants and feels, and listen; be there for him.
17. Lastly, even though he looks like a big, capable man, he lives in a world that doesn't make sense anymore. He finds the most comfort in reaching out and connecting to other people. When he was home, this got very dangerous. He would leave, go up to anyone, at any house or store, and would not stay home!
18. Please don't vilify his family by threatening to call and tell them what he did. This does nothing to help him. He won't remember. It just hurts him.

I'll bet you know almost all of this, and knowing that assures our family. I've seen you engage with Justin and the other residents sweetly and patiently. We all appreciate you enormously.

THANK YOU,
Kasey Claytor and Family

> I must include a mention of a few of the other dear residents Justin resided with. I was fond of and felt appreciation for so many of them. Like the dear woman who thought she was married to Donald Trump and would sit in the community room window watching for his limo to take her to dinner. Or the retired teacher who still used sarcasm to such perfection, you had to be impressed. Or the dear

woman who often walked the hallways with only her briefs, bra, and a smile. Or the surfer who pulled me aside asking if I'd bring him some pot. May they all be at peace wherever they are.

December 3, 2022

Justin is OK but getting into more trouble at his facility. It turns out it isn't working well to have him living with a lot of frail elderly folks. They keep getting into his room, which is annoying to him. Of course, they don't realize what they are doing. He keeps telling them to leave, but they don't understand, so he tries to help them out of his room. Dangerous! He likes his alone time.

He continues to have a food compulsion. Doc has tried everything drug-wise. He has now developed diabetes!!!!!! If his food is controlled, this should vastly improve. They can't do it where he is. They won't lock up the food for one resident and have him eat separately. It isn't their fault. They are all kind and doing their best.

We are moving him this Monday to a Traumatic Brain Injury facility for men 45 to 65. They lock up the food and dole out what is on his diet.

This happened when we planned on selling our home and downsizing to a house closer to Justin's facility, and I feel such exhaustion. Here we go again.

Kasey J. Claytor

December 12, 2022

Justin has been in the new facility since Monday, and we are encouraged. The residents are an interesting group, and the caregivers' ratio to residents is extraordinary. There are about eight residents and between 2 and 4 people on staff at all times. They are all experienced, mature, and kind to Justin and our family. One is nearing her degree, and one works weekends and teaches disabled children during the week. Most have been there a long time.

When I come in, they make me feel welcome, all smiles. Many of the residents, too! I miss the residents at the other place, but Justin fits in with these guys.

The administrator is warm and helpful. It is considered a home health care facility instead of a big facility with medical staff, so we are all learning new skills. I had to learn how to give Justin an insulin shot but as of yet, his blood sugar hasn't warranted it since arriving. I learned from his new pharmacist that some of the meds he is on can make diabetes more likely. Shout out to the Hobbs Pharmacy on Merritt Island. They have helped me so much. A huge benefit is the fact that they lock up the food, as I have noted, and keep the kitchen door and pantry locked. Each resident has a locker for approved snacks, and staff gives them some snacks during snack time. And it is closer to us! (Until we move!)

I got him another cell phone, as the last one went through the washer and dryer at the old place! It was in his jeans pocket. *The second time!* But his ability to use it has declined so much. We wanted to try it again so he could call or text. It's been minimal.

The night caregiver tucks him in at night, which warms my heart. This morning, she told me she took his comforter out of the dryer and covered him up when it was warm! (At the last facility, no one on the night shift bothered to check on him.)

The first day, we couldn't find him; we finally found him in the backyard in his underwear, trying to leave to go to the last memory care facility! But now he is *almost* totally accepting of the new place. He wakes up happy. The caregivers seem to like him.

December 19, 2022
To Nurse Danielle,
Where Justin Had Just Left

Sometimes, Christmas time is magical!

The staff at Justin's new place is great—caring, hardworking, inventive, and mature. It has made such a difference. The drawback is that no nurse is on staff; it is considered a home healthcare facility, so I had to learn how to give Justin insulin. But he hasn't needed a shot yet! His blood sugar is now below 100.

They have solved his problem of grabbing other residents' food. One of the staff members sits with him away from the main table and keeps him company while he eats. Then, they convince him to go to his room. And he does! He is losing weight, too!

It isn't anyone's fault this couldn't be done at your memory care. You don't have the staff to do this; he gets lots of compassionate attention.

You made a massive difference to us and are such a great person. I will miss you!!! Let's stay in touch because you never know what the future holds. XOXO

December 19, 2022

Rolling emotions sweep over me, positive ones and negative ones. I'm always anxious when a call comes in from Justin's facility. I need to work on that because it is often not bad news. But sometimes it is. He pushed someone. Someone hit him. Being around other men with brain issues with all the testosterone, some of the guys act out. And he's out of incontinence supplies; he needs more meds, etc.

I have been working on getting all his supplies on auto-reorder. I think it is done now, but getting it all worked out was quite time-consuming.

Then there is the theft. I suspected it at the previous places, but sometimes they'd find his missing items. Sometimes, they never showed up. Recently, Justin's phone went missing.

I placed a $50 bill in each of the staff's Christmas cards, and the administrator had to call me and tell me two cards were empty. I told her I knew each card had a 50-dollar bill. She said she would look at the camera from last Friday.

Then she called me Sunday night and told me one of the staff, a gentleman who seemed so personable and kind, could be seen taking the bills out of the Christmas cards. It was hard to believe. The admin was mortified it happened on her watch, and I asked what she would do. She said he'd have to be let go. It was somber in there this morning.

It strikes me sometimes that Justin's confounding condition is some kind of bad joke. Just when he gets settled and seems to be getting along, everything turns upside down again. His behavior, which he has no control over, is unpredictable and puzzling unless you note it is mainly like a three-year-old child. And I am faced with his stubbornness all over again. And the other residents getting aggressive with him, like the bullies in his childhood. It is like the 70s are back. Karma rules. It wasn't done yet.

Chapter 5: 2023

February 17, 2023
Newsletter to subscribers
from my coaching site.

I keep reading terrible descriptions of the condition, Frontotemporal Degeneration, which my older son has. Now that Bruce Willis has been diagnosed, more people will be aware of it, which will help fund more research. But the words used to describe it in support groups, websites, and posts are pretty horrific.

I don't see it as cruel or horrible. It just is, and when we don't look deeper at the possible divine causes beyond our ego, it *is* awful. But that's not healthy to think of it only in this way—to repeatedly complain and deconstruct the loved one's life in your mind. It treats your loved one and your family as permanent victims without available perspectives that enable you to rise to what I consider a healthier and more comforting perspective.

Every time I read these words like 'horrible' about FTD, it hurts like a paper cut. Yes, it is easy to describe a terminal illness like this. Especially while watching someone as they withdraw further from normal behavior.

I certainly will admit that it's hard to dig deeper into another perspective. And I feel deeply for all the suffering it causes to the families caring for the FTDer as well as those who have it. There is a lot we can do to lessen the suffering. For those who have someone in their life with FTD, you can find ways every day to make the FTDer right. Follow their emotions and try to understand what they are experiencing. Play music for them. Sit with them. Discover what interests them now.

When my son was in the early stages, we noticed he loved game shows and home video shows. So, we made sure he had those to watch.

The stages change gradually, so you need to, too. But as I've said, the emotions are still felt. Let that be your guide. Take nothing personally because they are not in control of what they say and do.

There is a deeper reality beyond our thinking mind, a cause we can't see yet, a purpose that may be hidden from us, a divine energy working within us, and it is more important than the symptoms and our descriptions. It is on this profound spiritual level of every family member and the FTDer, and one that can be sensed. Find that connection.

April 22, 2023

The administrator finally showed intolerance of Justin. She said she would need him to leave and gave us a timeline. I hurriedly pulled out my old, exhausted list of facilities and began calling and visiting other places once again. Most, of course, wouldn't take him because of his age.

It took me several weeks to find a place this time, and when I finally told the admin we were moving him, she said, "Oh, I changed my mind. He's fine to stay here!" I was dumbfounded. She hadn't bothered to tell me! Between you and me she was in over her head in her position. This home healthcare facility was privately owned, and there was no way to contact the owner. Suffice it to say there were red flags, and apparently, the owner had trouble finding someone more able to head the small TBI home. I do still wonder and worry about the ones left there.

We've been busy, moving from our river house about 20 miles south and Justin to a new facility on the beachside, closer to our new home. But we finally, finally, found the most wonderful place for him. Really!

I don't know where the energy to do all this comes from! Hopefully, things will calm down now.

Justin has declined quite a bit in the last two months. His meds have been adjusted a few times, and he's calm and mostly compliant. His communication has slowed down; he talks softly, and sometimes he uses the wrong words, so it is hard to comprehend what he means. The temporal brain, which is the communication center, is shrinking, making it hard for him to understand complex sentences and be understood.

Physically, he is much weaker. I often have to help pull him up out of my car. It is hard for him to remember where to place his feet to stand up. Once he is walking, he has no problem, but he walks slowly.

I had tried to get him on Hospice care before, but he was doing well physically, so they wouldn't take him. We need to try again now.

In an auspicious occurrence, another facility we were looking at advised us to go to this beachside place where he is now. I can't think of a better place for him at this stage. There is another FTD resident in memory care with him. There are three wanderers, Justin being one who likes to walk the halls. They have more licensed staff, more stimulating activities, good food, and sweet caregivers, and it is pleasant to go there.

It ended up being so bad where he was last. We want him to be somewhere he can stay permanently and are praying this is it.

A wise friend told me that Justin is in the process of 'letting go.' From our viewpoint, he seems to be slipping away, but under this friend's definition of letting go, he is slowly losing his worldly identification. This part holds our personality, judgments, ego drives, and all that has happened to us in our lives that shape our perspectives. What is left is his soul, his inner being, the core of who he is before and after this life. This is comforting. It is what I believe, and I sense his presence.

May 9, 2023

Justin is nearing the end of his journey here. We've anticipated this for four years, but there is no natural way to prepare for it. Even though we understand that he wouldn't want to continue in his current state, those who love him will still miss him terribly.

He is only slightly aware of what is happening when I come in. He can't swallow well anymore, so I hand-feed him his blended food. He is continually grateful, still. I do wonder where this comes from.

I came in one day to find him sitting in the activity circle, still drawn to be around others, even though walking down that hall was difficult; he was shuffling now. Yet, he was sitting and staring at the floor, unaware of the passing of the beach ball and unaware I was there. I sat on the floor before him and touched his knees. Startled, he opened his eyes wide with a big smile flashing across his face as he focused on me. A big "HI, MOM!" left his lips.

I smiled back; I welled up. The love I felt was overpowering.

I led him to his bed that day, and he lay down. I went into the bathroom to clean something, trying not to cry, and I heard steps beside me. I looked up, and Justin stood there, his arms outstretched to hug me. He hadn't done that in two years. Miraculous, mysterious. I've heard about dementia patients having moments of lucidity as they near the end of life, but that did not occur to me then.

My boy. Never, ever did he forget who I was. These were his last days. I knew to treasure them with all my heart.

Seven years ago, we lost a nephew, Jason, Bill's sister and brother-in-law's son. I think of them often and what they went through. I wrote something to read at Jason's funeral. I was trying to comfort and help all of us find peace. Now, I am clinging to my own words I wrote back then.

I'd like to share a portion of what I wrote:

"When we tap into the pain of losing a child, no matter what age they pass away, it is unconscionable. The pain is unfathomable. Even if we have solid, unflinching faith in the eternal life of the soul, in the infinite state of a being, the physical representation of that loved one we once held close, the one we delighted in, standing before us, the idea that he will be no more, is painful beyond imagination.

And yet, we are left here in this realm of physical life, without him in our reach, and we look at each other in our pain, not knowing where to place it. We look to each other for answers, guidance, and comfort. So here we are for this. It is all we can do: be here with each other.

Our hearts are broken open. But only a heart broken wide open can grasp the vastness of God's love. Only a heart broken wide open can glimpse a small piece of the divine love running through us all. It is greater than any one of us. But we are a part of it. We are made from it. And those we lost are one with it, as we will all be one day. When we hold this thought, we are near him."

So many have given me support, prayers, love, and kindness, which has fed me and made me feel nurtured and cared for. I know these last days of his life will be difficult, other-worldly, moving into uncharted territory. I pray I do everything that is needed for him and all of us. We must surrender, accept what is, allow the emotions to move through us, and realize love never dies.

And going through these difficult times leaves the residue of a much deeper understanding.

It is an understanding that may not be evident while going through this, yet we see it with new eyes down the road, and we are changed.

Finding the Light

Justin passed away May 16, 2023, on his father's birthday.

My good friend and fellow author wrote this poem in her book of poetry:

> Do not weep for me, my child,
> For I am free at last
> Of all of the encumbrances
> That held me in their grasp.
> Now my spirit freely soars,
> Released from all its pain.
> Transcendent joy is mine at last,
> Immortal love, my pure repast,
> So do not grieve, do not despair.
> Look in your heart - I will be there.

By Donna Meisbach, The Golden Hour, Selected Spontaneous Poem

I read both of these writings at Justin's memorial. Previous co-workers, current and past nurses who cared for Justin, family, and many friends came.

Kasey J. Claytor

November 5, 2023
Some musings on loss came to me during prayer and meditation.

There are two kinds of pain: the *love-pain* and the *self-pain*.

1. *Love-pain* is experienced when its source is deep love. In that love is exquisite pain that includes goodness.
2. *Self-pain* has no love source. It emerges out of a lack of love, which is suffering.

They both hurt. But one holds seeds of transcendence. One warns a change is needed; and, what happens as time goes by after losing someone dear? Does the grief get less? No, but the heart grows so much bigger than the grief that it is overtaken by the great love you've awakened to. How else could you know how much love you had/have?

He's With Me

He's with me
I know
When I listen to 'our' music station
He is with me
When I awake in the night thinking of him
He is with me
As I pray for him
He is with me
As surely as God is
I feel him
Love never dies

The following are excerpts from a newsletter I wrote to my subscribers on the best practices for navigating difficult times. It was written during Covid 2020.

6 Survival Tips for Rough Times

I recently made room in a filing cabinet for about 20 pounds of files for my son's care: finances, medical records, legal documents, disability insurance papers, health insurance, work records, address changes, and bills. The files are heavy both physically and emotionally, as I've carried them back and forth from home to work and work to home because I never knew when I'd need information in one of those folders. I'm in a window where I can temporarily put it down.

It is more important than ever to stop and recognize how we are doing, find what works and what doesn't, and help us maintain good physical and mental health in troubled times. Along with doing this for myself, I wanted to share it with all of you. Believe me, when I write recommendations like this, they are as much for me too!

My older son was diagnosed with Frontotemporal Degeneration, a mysterious brain disease that people, usually between 45 and 65, may be diagnosed with. I know of one afflicted with it who is only 26. Unlike Alzheimer's, it usually shows up with personality changes that can be so subtle that the affected person's family, though confused by some behavior, may miss the severity of the onset. Memory is eventually affected, and this disease includes dementia.

I tell you this because it has been highly challenging, and out of necessity, I must embrace all the skills, practices, and knowledge I've learned from following my interests in health—physical and emotional—and spiritually. I want to share a few pointers and suggestions to find some relief for yourself, especially if you ever get overwhelmed, irritated, sad, or depressed. Life can be hard.

I don't presume any of these ideas will bring you extraordinary normalcy or complete relief, but every small thing you can do to take care of yourself is important.

Here are my six suggestions, all of which I depend on at different times. I wouldn't like to wonder where I'd be without these practices. I think I'd be more anxious, with more profound sadness, harder to get along with, and less loving.

In brief:

1. Be easy on yourself and take care of each other
2. Create balance
3. Taking care of your physical self
4. Meditation and prayer
5. Be in the moment
6. Taking care emotionally/emotional intelligence

1. Be Easy on Yourself and Take Care of Each Other

We might all feel more irritable, anxious, or sad with all the problems these days. This makes it so easy for us to say things we don't mean to loved ones, make quick judgments without thinking, or pull away from others. Taking good care of ourselves enables us to be more patient and understanding with those feeling stressed. The best practice is to be quick to forgive yourself as well as others, start over, release those judgmental thoughts, and be present. Find a trick or a mantra to remind yourself when things begin to bother you. I've used "It doesn't matter" Or Om Nama Shivaya, which means surrender; I bow to everything—more on forgiveness in the section on emotional intelligence below.

When emotions grip you, find a moment to sit quietly and ask yourself where you sense this in your body. Your chest, gut, throat? Be present with the sensations without resisting them or repressing them. Give the feeling a label: I'm angry, I'm frustrated, etc. Ask silently what those sensations are telling you. They want acknowledgment! They usually slowly dissipate after the feelings have been recognized. You may find yourself doing this several times, and that is OK. That tightness, that ache, that pain, left unacknowledged, will become louder in another form if it is pushed away, ignored, or repressed; and think kindness. First to yourself and then others.

2. Create Balance

We need balance in our rest/activity, sleep/wake, balanced diet, and play/work.

When working on a project, on the computer, or doing chores, break it up with things you enjoy doing; reward yourself for each accomplished task.

Ayurvedic recommendations are an excellent reference. The premise of Ayurveda is to find balance in all ways.

Modern science has recently validated much of this body of knowledge, discovering the truths Ayurveda knew thousands of years ago.

According to Ayurveda, there are three main doshas or mind/body types, and everyone is a combination of these. I recommend going to the *Banyan Botanicals* website, banyanbotanicals.com, to take the quiz and find out your makeup and suggestions for a balanced diet and daily plan for your Dosha.

Get enough sleep. Go to bed by 10 or 10:30. Eat a light dinner, and don't eat past 7 p.m.

3. Taking Care of Your Physical Self

Walking is an excellent activity that is good for all body types. If you tend to be thin, you are most likely a Vata body type, and Hatha Yoga or some other slow, mindful exercise is best. Short spurts of more intense exercise are good if you are athletic and have good muscle formation. If you tend to be stocky and have good stamina, you can do just about any exercise. Please refer to your health providers before changing your routine. Once you learn your Dosha type, you can also check more recommendations on the Banyan website.

Another excellent way to reduce stress is massage. The benefits are well documented: mental relaxation, flushing of toxins, boosting of the immune system, and lymphatic drainage. We can also do it ourselves with a self-massage. I do this in about 5 minutes before jumping in the shower. Use a pleasant-scented natural oil and slowly massage your body, beginning at the scalp (or face if you aren't washing your hair).

For my Dosha, Vata/Pitta, I use cured sesame oil with a few drops of vetiver, sweet basil, and patchouli. To cure the oil, buy organic sunflower, sesame, or coconut oil and simmer until you see it churning. Add a drop of water, and it will pop when done. Don't let it boil. Allow it to cool before returning it to its bottle. Then, add the essential oil. More instructions are on the Banyan Botanicals site.

4. Prayer and Meditation

For me, this is essential. It is so easy to think you don't have time, or you can't stop your thoughts, or while sitting trying to meditate, you think of so many things you could be doing. But nothing will give you the same benefits as meditation. No matter how many times you've tried, know you can meditate.

The first rule is that you cannot do it wrong, and any 'trying' must be let go of. All it requires is sitting still on your chair or mat with your eyes closed or slightly open and gazing down. Everyone, even the most experienced meditators, has thoughts going through their minds. So what? Have a phrase or mantra to repeat over and over, and when you find you are deep into a story or other thoughts, stop and return your attention to the silent repetition of your mantra. It could be Let Go, Let God or Peace, Be Still, or any of the traditional mantras like So Hum.

My kaseyclaytor.com resources page includes a short discussion and instructions. There are also many guided meditations. Deepak Chopra has some excellent ones on YouTube and Facebook.

I admit I've experienced upheavals that hurt my daily practice, but looking back, the faster I could incorporate this practice into my life, the quicker my life reached a state of greater well-being.

Being a meditator doesn't mean your life becomes a smooth, completely pleasant one. Of course, events and situations pop up, like COVID, problems with other people, illness or hardships, and all the things we experience in daily life. But you may find that how you respond to these things is gradually changing.

You may find your highs during the day are a little higher, and your negative feelings come on perhaps not so strongly. Your irritation may come with more awareness. You might find yourself empathizing more easily and understanding on a deeper level. If you could graph your moods during the day—the highs and lows—you could see the shift, *which is a rise in consciousness.*

When I am knocked low by events I cannot control and my emotions erupt into a full-blown storm, even then, I know I have tools. There are things I can do immediately to lift some of the anxiety, anger, or sadness. Sometimes, it takes more than a few days to regain my balance, but so far, I always do.

As you learn to meditate, be easy with yourself. If you feel you failed or forgot to meditate, be gentle instead of self-condemning. Forgive yourself and start over.

5. Be in the Moment

Know this is temporary; practice presence.

"Everything will be okay in the end. If it's not okay, it's not the end." ~ John Lennon

Being in the moment is another way of saying to be mindful. It means that you pay complete attention to whatever you do instead of tuning in to the constant parade of worries about the future or lamenting over the past. Right now, you may have more than one problem in your life, or you are worrying about a loved one. Yet at this moment, while you're cutting vegetables, on an errand, opening mail, or paying bills, worrying at this moment isn't a bit productive. I knew a counselor who called this disaster planning.

I put that concern on an imaginary elevator of my mind, up and away, maybe even writing it down. Then I go back to chopping those vegetables in a mindful, totally present way, and, as often happens, later, with a clear mind, a solution to that problem will emerge.

When we are focused on our inner stories—what will happen, how bad things are, what happened in the past—not only are we missing the beauty of this moment of life, but we are sending fight-or-flight hormones throughout our bodies. Every cell is listening to your emotional state, your anxiety heralding warnings to brace for some unknown enemy with perfectly orchestrated reactions, and every system is affected. When this becomes a constant state, it inevitably affects your well-being in small or big ways.

Being in the moment, mindful right now, reverses all that. There are so many things we can do to shift this. Moving our attention from our thoughts and minds to bodily sensations is big. Yoga is excellent for this, as is mindful walking, most sports, or delving into your passions: a hobby or creative activity like quilting, writing, drawing, building things, or anything that focuses on the here and now. Peace Be Still.

6. Emotional Intelligence

What is emotional intelligence? Whether you're using this term as an attribute, as part of a person's character, maturity, or another quantifier, we instinctively know that the more emotionally aware and knowledgeable we are about what we or other people are feeling, the better we are at dealing with difficult emotions.

Like Dr. David Hawkins's consciousness studies and Ken Wilbur's Integral Psychology theory, there must be a graduating scale upon which we find our level of understanding of ourselves and the world. The more we understand, the more aware we are of our motivations and others, and the easier it is to overcome strong, unpleasant emotions.

Haven't you been so upset at another person or situation that your peace was destroyed? Your thoughts about it cause unpleasant, visceral reactions in your body, affecting your sleep and making you irritable, sad, or anxious. It is like a dark mood has taken over your whole being. While blaming someone, blaming yourself, or trying to repress it, you can't move past it. Eventually, something has to give; hopefully, it isn't causing more drama or creating an imbalance in your body.

One of the most significant signs that you are gaining emotional intelligence is realizing that what makes you miserable isn't so much the situation or the behavior of another as your reaction to it. So, how do we move into this? One of the tools I find essential for getting a handle on this is Byron Katie's *The Work*.

It is a worksheet you can print from her site or download as an app on your phone. It moves you through steps that help you see the situation or the other person from a new perspective. I highly recommend it for those stuck in their drama.

When strong emotions overcome you, when you are feeling down, angry, or sad, these feelings are held within your body. See the instructions in number one above for the exercise suggested to let these emotions dissipate.

Forgive yourself and others. This can be hard, I know. It is often harder to forgive oneself than others. Emotional intelligence also includes giving yourself love. Find ways to be loving to yourself. We hear all the time, *Love Yourself*. But how do you do that? With forgiveness, showing yourself loving kindness, allowing yourself to fail, taking breaks, declining things that pose more stress, and giving yourself the gift of ease, making it easier on yourself. I've found Catherine Ponder's prayer on forgiveness helpful over the years.

Emotional intelligence also includes knowing who is good for you to be around, who isn't, and who to invite into your world. This is another way of being in tune with your gut reactions to others and what they say. One of the difficult things about having a serious situation like my son's illness is confiding in others, and their reactions end up causing more hurt.

They are trying to help, but, especially with those of us who are educated in one of the many alternative health modalities, sometimes a person I am talking to will give me unsolicited advice on an exhausting list of research, things to look up, things to try, until I feel sick inside, and it makes my head hurt.

My reaction is, *oh, my God, I'm not doing enough,* or *I'm doing it wrong,* etc. I then have to step back and work out of those feelings because I know I am doing as much as possible to maintain my son's and my healthy balance. Sometimes, of course, people respond simply, I'll pray, or I feel your pain, which is helpful. And sometimes, I do ask for advice, especially from professionals and friends who have experienced something similar.

Also, when our tools fail, our practices are ineffective, and our emotions create too much pain, it's a good idea to call professional help. I wish more people understood mental health counseling. We, unfortunately, have a resistance in our culture, many believing it is a weakness to seek a therapist. We benefit from those who are well-known for being open about their therapy. I watched the other day a CNN announcer who shared how something he had learned in therapy helped him. Many problems with anxiety, depression, or obsessive behavior are responsive to a few weeks of sound therapy.

Dr. Chopra often talks about our existential angst, which originates in our most basic fear, the fear of loss of our ego, the fear of death. The fear of death is at the base of all fears. When we discuss all the negative emotions and problems we face, it helps to remember that there is no way we can be harmed at the spiritual level. We spring from our Source, God, infinite, non-physical Divine Love, and all unfolds for our greater good. We are evolving and expanding in each moment with greater potential. Connecting to our spiritual self will bring the assuredness of our invincibility.

Epilogue

How do I tie all this together when this experience with my son changed every disparate piece of my life, from my emotions and psyche to my spirit?

When tragedy enters our lives, it is overwhelming. It is hard to see clearly, understand the whys, and reach a place of comfort again.

When putting these writings together, I received several inspired thoughts. Whether during meditation or a prodding wake-up in the middle of the night, a paragraph or two would flood into my mind, fully formed. I'm sure other writers experience this. And if I didn't reach for a pen and paper and write it down, it would evaporate soon after.

These paragraphs usually explain a perspective that had eluded me before, with a more spiritual understanding of the events surrounding Justin's condition. My normal, worldly mind stumbled to find answers to what was happening. I believe these messages are true gifts from God, my inner-being, angels, or higher self; fill in according to your beliefs.

Even words out of Justin's mouth were, at times, magical and mysterious, simple yet true. I look back at those last years with him with wonder. As we drove on his favorite winding road along the river and I'd see him smiling, I was often overcome with the awareness of how temporary it was. How precious and love-filled these times were, holding me in deep gratitude mixed with pain. The pain was about the future I would face without him. Yet I now have the comforting memories of his happiness.

I would look out over the water and say, "What a beautiful day!"

And he would smile at me, saying, "Yes, and you are beautiful too!" as I tried to hide my tears.

"It's a great day!", "It is very important to be a good person." "We should not be prejudiced." "You are BME, the Best Mom Ever!" and "I love you, Mom."

"(Nurse's name) is very nice. I told her I loved her."

For those touched by dementia, whether you are caring for someone with FTD or you have been diagnosed with it, it's important to find ways to make it easier on yourself. Accept help, find breaks, and talk with counselors and experts. And know this is not your fault.

There are hard times when you feel you have no control and everything is going in the wrong direction. But there are also times when glimmers of light and love shine through. Both are part of the journey. See if you can step back from what is happening outside and try to connect with the grander mystery of life. Also, find those times that are peaceful when it feels like all is well. They will come. When they do, fill yourself up with them, relaxing into this light. Justin would say, it is a good day.

Acknowledgments

I want to thank and acknowledge all the help, support, and kindness from those in our lives during this journey with Justin:

To Justin himself, he is my teacher—ever loving and forgiving, no matter what I did or said. I am so imperfect as a parent. In his apparent illness, he was a genius; he was light.

My husband, Bill, who has always believed in me, loved and supported me, and made sure I had a warm meal waiting at home, consistently picking up any slack from my absence while I was with Justin.

My son, Aaron, showed amazing love for his older brother, which still amazes me today. To see his tender care for Justin blew me away. He stepped up in the biggest way.

To my sister-in-law Geralyn, who made it her mission to visit Justin regularly as a fun-loving aunt. They had such a good time together.

To his cousin Todd, who helped me with Justin's sweet chickens.

To cousin Krista, who supported me from California and came home for his birthday.

To Terri Boekhoff, who never gave up on our search for facilities for Justin and spent hours on the phone for us.

To Danielle Torres, a compassionate, wonderful nurse Justin truly loved. She always made a big effort to understand him.

To Donna Bogan, another exceptional nurse who was there until the end. I so wish I'd known her sooner. With her humor and wisdom, she is terrific.

To Dr. Shane Hernesman was available anytime, any day for Justin and answered my endless questions, requests, and concerns.

To Kathy Vital, Dr. Hernesman's assistant and receptionist, with whom I spent endless hours on the phone. Her help and support were invaluable.

To Dr. Vijay Jain, whose care, concern, and suggestions were so helpful to us, especially Justin. He loved taking his Pitta pills!

To Chaplin Matthew Kern and St. Francis Hospice, who hung in there with me at the end, providing spiritual support, loving care, and most of all, listening to me anytime I needed to talk, even to this day.

To Brent BecVar, who kept reminding me to be present with Justin and to stick with the spiritual practices that helped me maintain my sanity.

To Sandi Lutz, my theaftd.org counselor, who was always available to listen and tell me stories about how others had gone through this journey.

Finding the Light

To Matt Ozga and theaftd.org for all the resources and support throughout Justin's condition.

To Scott Lanford, my attorney, who put all this aside to help us prepare for Justin's situation.

To Karma Malone, who worked in human resources where Justin worked and helped us navigate his termination and apply for benefits.

To Liam Steinberg of our partners, Efficient Advisors, who miraculously helped us with Justin's assets at work.

To Roxann Morin, who worked with me tirelessly to finish a book that had been put aside as I took care of Justin.

To Gayle Harrison, Justin's first caregiver, who was loving and kind to him.

I want to thank my dearest friends, Dawn Lopez, Elyse Hope Killoran, and Julie Schueler, for their loving support. A special thank you to Dawn Lopez, who has always read everything I've written and given me honest and good suggestions.

To Donna Miesbach, such an important mentor, advisor, friend, and editor in my life!

To Mark Anthony, who always reminds me Justin is fine, still near and at peace.

To Myong Tober, Justin's friend and co-worker, who took the time to visit Justin several times.

To Joanne Cooper at the credit union, who helped us so much with all the financial tasks we had to do.

And to Winn and Monica, who were Justin's first caregivers at the first facility and came to visit Justin and take him for rides after he moved out.

Bibliography

6 Survival Tips for Caregiving and Stress, 121
10 Caregiving Rules When Caring for Those with Dementia, 68
A Place for Mom, 49
Ayurveda, 63, 94, 123
Banyan Botanicals, 124
Byron Katie and *The Work*, 129
Catherine Ponder and Forgiveness, 129
Contented Dementia, by Oliver James, 33, 36, 102
CCF Tea, 39
Chopra, Dr. Deepak, 126
GPS Tracker, 42
Legal Documents, 28
Meditation, 125
Neurology Today Article About Overeating and FTD, 96
SSDI, 28

Poems:
Today Justin is OK, 31
When the Brain Won't Oblige, 51
Morning Ride, 91
Do Not Weep for Me, 119
He's With Me, 120

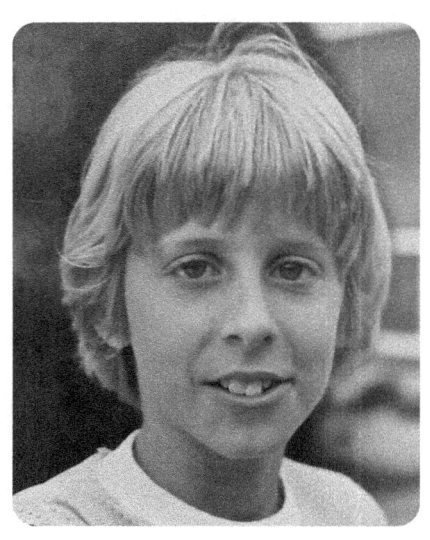

Justin Michael Wade
June 24, 1970 – May 16, 2023

www.ingramcontent.com/pod-product-compliance
Lightning Source LLC
Chambersburg PA
CBHW070459100426
42743CB00010B/1683